The Universities
of Europe, 1100–1914

The Universities
of Europe, 1100–1914

A History

Willis Rudy

Rutherford • *Madison* • *Teaneck*
Fairleigh Dickinson University Press
London and Toronto: Associated University Presses

Associated University Presses
440 Forsgate Drive
Cranbury, N.J. 08512

Associated University Presses
25 Sicilian Avenue
WC1A 2QH, England

Associated University Presses
2133 Royal Windsor Drive
Unit 1
Mississauga, Ontario, Canada L5J 1K5

Library of Congress Cataloging in Publication Data

Rudy, Willis, 1920–
 The universities of Europe, 1100–1914.

 Bibliography: p.
 Includes index.
 1. Universities and colleges—Europe—History.
I. Title.
LA627.R82 1984   378.4   82-49281
ISBN 0-8386-3177-0

Printed in the United States of America

To the memory of my mother and father,
and to Dorothy

Contents

Preface

"A university," writes Eric Ashby, "is a mechanism for the inheritance of the Western style of civilization. It preserves, transmits, and enriches learning, and it undergoes evolution as animals and plants do."[1] In short, the university is the key institution devised by Western civilization for the advancement of knowledge and the training of society's most highly skilled workers. Originating in the European Middle Ages, it has become the primary vehicle in all parts of the world for the preservation and transmission of the highest learning, the advancement of scholarship, the training of specialists in fields of endeavor vital to society, and the improvement of national life.

The purpose of this volume is to review the main currents in the historical evolution of the university in its European homeland. This course of development is traced down to 1914, by which time the main outlines of the contemporary university had taken shape. The emphasis throughout this study is on the most central and significant patterns of university growth as seen in the context of the times in which they occurred. For this reason no exhaustive excursions have been made into special aspects such as student folkways and living patterns or the lives of eminent professors.

Preface

The history of universities constitutes one of the most important and exciting chapters in the history of world civilization. Some years ago, Hans Kohn asserted that "our time is dominated by a feeling of unprecedented crisis involving every aspect of political, social, and intellectual life."[2] It is my hope that this overview of the history of the university will have positive value in our time of crisis for those who have an active concern for civilization's present and future.

1

The First Universities

Higher learning existed long before the first universities made their appearance. The scribes and priests of ancient Egypt and Babylon pursued advanced studies and carefully preserved their own forms of higher learning as early as the second millenium B.C.[1] Many centuries later the academies, lyceums, and gymnasia of ancient Greece developed a system of higher education that is generally considered to be the foundation of western civilization.[2] Greek learning subsequently spread throughout the Mediterranean and Near East during the Hellenistic era (330–100 B.C.).[3] When Rome later conquered much of the then-known world, the already well-established Greek pattern of higher learning continued to be the most influential model.[4]

With the downfall of the Roman empire, many higher intellectual pursuits were seriously undermined or interrupted, but the traditions of Greek and Roman higher learning were maintained vigorously at Byzantium, the capital of the Eastern empire.[5] The spread of Islam, beginning in the seventh and eighth centuries A.D., also played an important role in the wide diffusion of higher learning throughout the Mediterranean area and the Near East. Muslim centers from Cordova in Spain to Baghdad in Mesopotamia quickly absorbed much of the Graeco-Roman learning, translated it into Arabic, and elaborated upon it extensively. By A.D. 1100 scholars from all parts of Latin Europe were coming to study this significant body of recovered knowledge (known as "the new Aristotle") in the thriving Muslim schools of Spain.[6]

Higher learning thus had flourished for at least three millennia before the first European universities were established. But significant as they were in their own right, the Academy of Athens, the Museum of Alexandria, and the House of Learning of Baghdad were not true universities. For authentic universities to exist (in the modern meaning of that term), there must be permanent institutions of learning employing regular teaching staffs, offering specific courses of higher studies, administering examinations from time to time, and granting certificates of accomplishment in the form of generally recognized diplomas or degrees. Not until the later Middle Ages did institutions emerge on the historical scene which met these specifications by embodying all of the above-mentioned characteristics.

Origins of the Medieval Universities

A long period of time elapsed—some six centuries—between the dark days when the last of the great academies of antiquity were shut down and the exciting times when the first universities began their work. During this lengthy interlude, higher education in the West survived only as a result of the efforts of Church agencies such as monasteries and cathedrals. The first churchmen of those days to play an active role in intellectual life were rural-based monks, members of the "regular" clergy. These churchmen maintained important schools and libraries such as those at Monte Cassino, the famed monastery of the Benedictines. Learned monks were also active in the Carolingian Renaissance of the eighth and ninth centuries A.D.

As time went on, however, most of the initiative in education was taken over by the more urbanized "secular" clergy. In contrast to the cloistered monks, the secular clergy had assumed a responsibility to minister to the outside world and were deeply involved in the life of the reviving towns. As they grew in number, schools multiplied in their churches, especially in the great cathedrals. Individual masters and lecturers began to appear at these urban schools, and some developed a widespread reputation for knowledge. Students flocked to the cathedral towns to hear them. By the twelfth century the need for some form of organization and control to ensure protection of these teachers and students was becoming obvious.

John B. Mullinger observes that "the early universities rose in response to new wants."[7] These wants, in turn, were stimulated by new circumstances in Europe. What were these circumstances? First of all, by the twelfth century European intellectual horizons were being broadened as a result of post-Crusades contacts with the Muslim civilizations and the Byzantine empire. A "veritable explosion of knowledge" was occurring as the "new Aristotle" and other rediscovered and newly translated ancient works were assimilated and the study of Roman law was revived. At the same time, the western European economy began to expand and town life became vigorous once again. With the revival of towns and trade came the development of a well-defined guild and corporate structure as the primary form of social organization. (The first universities emerged as yet another form of medieval corporation.) In addition, the increasingly complex society of the later Middle Ages had a great need for trained administrators, lawyers, notaries, physicians, and ecclesiastics. Such people had to secure their advanced training somewhere. The cathedral schools at such places as Chartres, Orléans, Rheims, Laon, York, and Salisbury were the first educational institutions to seek to satisfy their needs. They were soon put in the shade by the enormous reputation of the cathedral school of Paris, where teachers such as William of Champeaux and Pierre Abelard drew large numbers of enthusiastic students. The first steps toward the creation of universities had been made.

Salerno. It is difficult to give precise dates for the foundation of the first medieval universities because they usually arose spontaneously as a result of the gatherings of scholars or the teaching of some charismatic figure. Such was certainly the case at Salerno in southern Italy, a "meeting-place of Greek, Latin, Arabic and Jewish culture."[8] As early as the ninth century A.D., the place was renowned for its health resort and its many skilled physicians. Some of the most prominent physicians began to teach there about that time, and Salerno came to be widely celebrated for its medical instruction. The chief textbooks were translated ancient classics, such as the works of Hippocrates and Galen, Jewish writings including the books of Isaac Judaeus, and Muslim commentaries, such as those of Avicenna. Begun informally, Salerno finally gained official state recognition in 1231 as a "university," but even then remained solely a medical school.

Bologna. In the northern Italian towns rhetoric and law schools that had flourished in Roman times possibly never went out of existence completely during the chaotic years that followed. By the middle ages, the Lombard cities of

the north Italian plain were developing a lively civic per-
sonality and a marked political autonomy, largely as a
result of their ability to play off the Holy Roman Empire
against the Papacy. Their relatively free political structure
was undergirded by commercial prosperity. Rashdall com-
pares them to the city-states of ancient Greece. In these
bustling *municipia*, mature students came from distant
towns for specialized professional training in practical avoc-
ations such as law. As early as the eleventh century,
Pavia, Ravenna, and Bologna had emerged as the best
places to obtain such advanced instruction. Of all these
legal centers Bologna became the most famous, perhaps
because it was a natural crossroads of northern Italy, a
place where all the main routes converged. A municipal
school dating back to Roman times was in operation there.
The town also boasted a diocesan school for the study of
the arts and a monastic school devoted to the canon
(church) law.

Famous teachers appeared there, too, such as Irnerius
and Gratian. Irnerius, a learned legal scholar, was a citizen
of Bologna who had originally been a protégé of the papal
party. He switched sides, however, and became an apolo-
gist for the emperor. In the early twelfth century he con-
ducted a school in Bologna for the study of the civil law,
using as the main source Emperor Justinian's great compi-
lation of Roman law—the *corpus juris civilis*. Gratian, by
contrast, was a Benedictine monk attached to the monastery of St. Felix in Bologna. His masterwork, a monumen-
tal concordance of all known church or canon laws, came
to be known as the *Decretum Gratiani*. Gratian's reputation
drew to Bologna many students and scholars interested in
the developing field of ecclesiastical law and even gained
the attention of the Papacy, which saw in this area of
knowledge a powerful legal weapon for use in its increasingly bitter conflict with the imperial authorities.[9]

The subsequent *studium* (place of study) of Bologna

developed gradually out of these flourishing legal studies. The law students at Bologna were on the whole mature and financially independent. Most of them were foreigners, however, while most of the teachers (masters) were Bolognese citizens. To be an alien in a medieval city was no small thing. It meant that no matter how eminent one's family back home, one lived under harsh discriminatory laws and taxes. Christopher Driver points out that university statutes elsewhere in Italy specify frequently that scholars have the privilege to be exempt from torture except in the presence of and with the approval of the university rector.[10] There were other potential abuses lying in wait for aliens: avaricious landlords, heavy municipal taxes, compulsory militia service. How were the students, as outlanders, to defend themselves against such impositions? Organization was the obvious answer, for it would enable them to make use of a form of collective bargaining. Organization plus the threat of withdrawal would dramatize to the municipality and its leaders the commercial advantages that Bologna would lose should the students decide to leave in a body.

The organization that the law students at Bologna resorted to in order to defend their interests was, in essence, the university of Bologna. In the early twelfth century, they formed student guilds, modeled on the other corporate organizations that were customary in the economic and social life of medieval towns; these guilds were known as *universitates*. These student guilds (the equivalent, in some ways, of modern trade unions) were in turn subdivided on ethnic and regional grounds into four "nations." By 1195 these groups had been merged into two great student universities, the ultramontane (non-Italians) and the cismontane (Italians). Organized under their own leaders, or rectors, the students readied themselves for a confrontation, if necessary, with the commune (municipal government) of Bologna or with the law school masters (the latter eventually formed their own guild, the *collegium doctorum*, in 1215).[11]

The students had already received help from the imperial government, at least on paper. In 1158 German Emperor Frederick Barbarossa, courting support from the scholarly community for his position *vis à vis* the Papacy and the north Italian communes, issued a *Privilegium Scholasticum*, sometimes referred to as the *Authentica habita*. This proclamation extended imperial protection to all persons traveling into or out of Italy for purposes of study. There is no evidence, however, that the emperor had the power to enforce his sweeping pronunciamento within the confines of Bologna or any other self-governing Italian city. Nor could the law students easily turn to the church for help, for, unlike those enrolled in cathedral schools, most of them were civilians and therefore lacked whatever protection "benefit of the clergy" might afford.[12]

The Bologna student *universitates* decided finally that the only way they could secure the measure of control they desired over the local *studium* and protect their rights as individuals was to resort to direct action. To secure the concessions they demanded, they simply withdrew in a body from the town in 1217. They stayed away for three years, which was bound to have an impact on the Bolognese economy, and finally the Commune and the masters had to give in. The students were granted concessions on such things as rents, food prices, and local taxes. They were also accorded exemption from military service. The masters agreed to recognize the authority of the student guilds as independent *universitates* with the right, in essence, to appoint their own teachers and to prescribe in detail the procedures these lecturers were to follow in presenting their material. Thus, Bologna had in the early thirteenth century, established the vital precedents that would be followed by all future student-dominated universities. The Bolognese masters were not completely powerless, however. They still retained the right to examine and admit members of their own guild and, in connection with this, they had the power to either grant or withhold the *licentia docendi* (license or degree) in canon or civil law that signified the formal admission of an individual to the legal profession.[13]

Paris. The university of Paris, like that at Bologna, was never founded, as such, at a particular moment; instead it slowly evolved, spontaneously, out of the cathedral school that already existed in the town. Unlike Bologna, however, Paris was not a self-governing commune but the capital city of the French monarchy and the seat of an important bishopric. And unlike the teachers in Bologna, the Paris masters found themselves in a considerably stronger bargaining position with respect to their students, who tended to be much younger and less independent than their counterparts in the Italian city.

Students flocked in growing numbers to Paris after 1100 A.D. to study logic and dialectic with famous masters in preparation for careers as theologians. John of Salisbury, returning to England in the middle of the twelfth century after a visit to the French capital, reported that "all learned Paris had gone well-nigh mad in its pursuit and practice of the new dialectic."[14] Scholastic controversies between such figures as Lanfranc and Berengar (and later, Anselm and Roscelinus), together with the deepening struggle between the nominalists and the realists, only added to the excitement.

The increasingly numerous and influential "artists," as the Paris masters teaching the *artes liberales* were known, decided eventually to follow customary practice and set up a guild, or *universitas*, to protect their mutual interests. Precisely when this happened is not known, but it may have occurred sometime between 1150 and 1175. Their guild was known as the *universitas magistrorum Parisiensis*. These masters taught at a *studium*, which had evolved from the earlier cathedral school of Paris. Later, when it received a papal charter, it was known as a *studium generale* (general place of study). It wasn't until the fifteenth century that people began to use the term *universitas* as a synonym for *studium*, with the latter name gradually falling into disuse. Long before that time, however, those scholars who studied and taught one particular field or subject came to be referred to as a "faculty," a term derived from the medieval Latin *facultas*, meaning a strength or power to do certain specific things, and therefore an appropriate designation for the various subject-matter divisions of the teacher's guild.[15]

After getting their *licentia docendi* from the archbishop's representative–the chancellor of the cathedral, the masters set up school on the crowded island of the Cité. There, they were to be found near the bridges connecting the island with the "left bank," or sometimes across the river in the left-bank neighborhood (called the "Latin quarter" because the language of scholars predominated there), not far from the great abbey of Sainte-Genevieve. About 1200, the masters put the by-laws that they had drawn up to govern their guild (the equivalent of university statutes) into writing. These prescribed a stated academic dress, enforced decorum at lectures and disputations, and required attendance at members' funerals.[16]

Meanwhile, a battle royal was brewing between the masters and the chancellor. The masters insisted that the chancellor recognize the corporate existence of their guild and grant teaching licenses only to those qualified persons who had been approved by their organization. In modern terminology, the masters demanded a closed shop for their trade union. The chancellor, who served as the equivalent of superintendent of schools for the diocesan authorities, rejected these demands out of hand. He regarded them as the insolent pretensions of upstart teachers; their supposed organization he viewed as unlawful and insubordinate—a "conspiracy" against the archbishop, who was the rightful superior of these malcontents. Furthermore, the chancellor and the cathedral chapter suspected that the unsupervised masters constituted a corps of unorthodox instructors, the propagators of all kinds of doctrinal license. A profound impasse ensued while the masters were involved in prolonged litigation with the chancellor and the cathedral chapter. The master's university was obliged now to raise money for expenses and to take certain other measures as a corporation, including the adoption of a common seal and the election of officers (known as proctors). Members of the Faculty of Arts, the youngest and most militant section of the university, took the lead in carrying the fight to the chancellor. A number of them, to make their point, withdrew from the island completely and set up schools on the left bank on what came to be known as the Rue de Fouarre (Straw Street, so named because students sat on the straw used there for a floor covering in these unheated quarters). There, they sought to create a rival to the chancellor, obtaining teaching licenses from the abbot of Sainte-Genevieve.[17]

The only supreme court that could settle this dispute was the Holy See in Rome, since most of the Paris masters, like the chancellor and diocesan staff, technically had the status of *clerici* (members of the clergy). The Papacy, jealous of the pretensions of the local episcopal authorities, was quick to throw its support behind the claims of the Paris university. The Holy See in 1212 forbade the chancellor to exact an oath of obedience from the masters or to refuse a teaching license to any candidates recommended by the masters in the several faculties. The chancellor was also forbidden to imprison or fine any of the scholars. At first, the Paris diocese refused to submit to the papal decrees. The chancellor excommunicated the university *en masse* for conspiracy and denied its right to make statutes. The masters stood firm, however, and so did the Papacy, and finally the chancellor was forced to yield.[18]

Further privileges for the Paris university came as a result of town *vs.* gown riots and threats of *cessatio* (moving the institution out of town). The latter strategy was relatively easy to implement in the early days of the university when it had no endowments to speak of and no permanent buildings of its own. Many of the classes at this time were held in rented buildings or borrowed churches and chapter houses along the Rue de Fouarre.

The universities very quickly emerged as pawns in the power struggles between the Papacy and local episcopal authorities and between the Papacy and secular rulers such as the national monarchs and the Holy Roman Emperor. King Philip Augustus of France was uneasy at the growing tendency of the Holy See to assume jurisdiction over these newly important educational institutions. Hence he reacted swiftly when a serious riot that involved the Paris university broke out in 1200. The servant of a wealthy and influential German student was thrown out of a tavern after making uncomplimentary remarks about the quality of the wine served there. In retaliation, a group of German students descended on the tavern and beat up the innkeeper. Soon thereafter, a mob of Paris townsmen assembled and led by the provost of the city (the leader of the municipality), launched retaliatory attacks upon the student culprits, killing several of them. The masters immediately appealed to the king for redress, threatening *cessatio*. Philip Augustus, seeing an opportunity to counter the Papacy's influence over the university community and fearing that a scholarly exodus would withdraw an important source of business and revenue from Paris, quickly granted their request. The guilty provost was removed from his position and imprisoned for life and, even more important, the Crown agreed to issue a charter to "the Scholars of Paris" in which the king recognized the students' rights as *clerici* to be tried only in ecclesiastical courts. All Parisians were commanded to respect the privileges of the scholars and all future provosts of Paris were required to take an oath, in the presence of the masters, promising to do likewise. Members of the university and students were exempt now from taxation and from arrest by the royal police for anything short of capital offenses.[19]

These were important gains for the Parisian scholars, involving as they did recognition of their status as specially privileged subjects. As Rashdall is careful to point out, however, these concessions were strictly limited insofar as they pertained to the university as a corporate entity. The privileges were granted, not to the scholar's guild as such, but to the masters and students as individuals. And the rights that were specified by the king, especially the immunities from secular justice, were already enjoyed by the scholars as "clerks" (*clerici* entitled to "benefit of the clergy").[20] Moreover, there were ancient precedents for Philip Augustus's actions. "Provisions for the conferring of special favors or privileges on those who taught" may be traced all the way back to the first century A.D. and were incorporated in the civil law codes of imperial Rome.[21]

For the university itself to secure the full chartered rights it desired, it was obvious that outside intervention would be necessary, most likely by the Papacy. It took another riot and a full-blown university strike to bring this about. In 1229, a group of students on vacation found some "most excellent and smooth wine" in a tavern and consumed rather too much of it. A dispute over the bill ensued and the young men were finally thrown out by the tavern keeper. The students returned with reinforcements, broke up the wine casks, and having become inordinately "flown with insolence and wine," took "indecent liberties . . . with peaceable *bourgeois* and *bourgeoises*." When this was reported to Queen Blanche, she quickly ordered the provost and his police to punish the guilty scholars, which task these guardians of the law performed so enthusiastically that they indiscriminately killed a number of young men and wounded many others. The arts masters promptly demanded redress once again from the Crown. Receiving none this time, they were obliged to resort to their ultimate weapon—*cessatio*. The members of the arts faculty at the University of Paris simply went on strike; they withdrew from the city *en masse* and dispersed to various other communities. The strike lasted three years. The theology teachers, meanwhile, refusing to support the strike, stayed at their posts. Pope Gregory IX, anxious to have the whole university reassembled and sensing an opportunity to increase his influence over it, recalled his cardinal legate from France, demanding that the civil authorities punish the offending police. Moreover he issued a bull, *Parens scientiarum* (Mother of Sciences), in 1231 that constituted, in effect, the long-desired charter for the university.[22]

The University of Paris, then, had emerged by 1231 as a fully chartered corporate entity under papal protection, secure from various kinds of interference by local church authorities or civil government. But in return for this protection the pope had spelled out in detail the rules to which the masters and students were expected to conform. In return for this obedience, the pope authorized the Paris masters to award the full rights of *jus ubique docendi*, meaning that the holders of its degree were recognized as having a license to teach anywhere in Christendom. Pope Gregory wished to establish the precedent here that only universities possessing a charter from the Holy See had the right to award such a degree. In any event, the University of Paris, after many vicissitudes, had at last won recognition of its corporate existence and was by this time electing its common officers, using a common seal, and conducting business as a legal entity. As a result of the leading role played by the masters in the fight to establish its rights, Paris had gradually emerged as a masters' (teacher-dominated) educational institution in sharp contrast to Bologna, and as such was to play a significant role in influencing the administrative structure of most future universities in northern Europe and North America.[23]

The Proliferation of Universities

The disputes that led to migrations and secessions at the first European universities ultimately led, by a sort of chain reaction, to the establishment of many new ones. Rashdall believes that "half the universities of Europe originated in migrations of this kind from older universities."[24] Secessions from Bologna led to the founding of a whole group of universities in northern Italy. Vicenza may have been set up in this way as early as 1202; Padua certainly did begin in 1222 by this means. In turn, Vercelli emerged in 1228 as the result of a secession from Padua. All of these institutions were civic or municipal enterprises, often seeking to attract business and increase the town's population. In addition to those already mentioned, civic *studia* were established at Reggio, Perugia, Piacenza, Verona, Pisa, Florence, Siena, Modena, Arezzo, and Pavia in the thirteenth and fourteenth centuries, all more of less on the Bolognese model. In Spain, universities of a very similar type appeared at Palencia, Salamanca, and Valladolid, while Coimbra was founded in Portugal. In Rome, Pope Innocent IV established a *studium* in 1245 closely dependent upon the papal court.[25]

Paris was the great model for the proliferating universities of northern Europe, as Bologna was for the south. In the thirteenth century, Angers was founded by refugees from Paris, and Orléans, Lyons, and Rheims were patterned after the school in the French capital. Montpellier, the successor to Salerno as a center of medical education, followed a more independent path, however. In England, Oxford was modeled closely on Paris, and Cambridge was founded around 1208 by scholars who had been obliged to flee from Oxford after a bloody town *vs.* gown riot. Cantabrigian numbers were later increased by the *cessatio* (1229–1231) from Paris.[26]

After 1225, more and more universities were established, not by refugee scholars, but by the rulers of various lands as part of the grand strategy of medieval power politics. A good example of this trend was the founding of the University of Naples in 1224 by Holy Roman Emperor Frederick II in order to train officials and lawyers for the imperial administration and to rival the influence of the pro-Papacy *(Guelf)* University of Bologna, which was at that time serving the interests of the hostile Lombard League. Naples was the first university established by imperial decree. Similarly, the University of Toulouse was created in 1229 by Count Raymond VII, with papal encouragement, for the specific purpose of combating the Albigensian heresy in the south of France and recapturing that area for the church and its secular allies. In England at about the same time, Oxford emerged as an unmistakably national enterprise, its origins going back to Becket's quarrel with King Henry II. As the dispute between England

and France became severe, the English students in Paris were recalled "from the domain of their king's enemy." It was then, with the Crown's encouragement, that at this central point for all south and west England, a great *studium* was established whose fame soon rivaled that of Paris and Bologna.[27]

Later, during the Hundred Years War, both the French and English governments sponsored universities with the aim of stirring up public sentiment in their favor. And in the fifteenth century, when the University of Paris began to support the claims of the French hierarchy to substantial independence from the Holy See, the Papacy retaliated by encouraging the establishment of rival universities at Nantes and Bourges. Other universities created by the state as acts of national policy included Prague (1347), Cracow (1362), Vienna (1365), and Heidelberg (1386). Similar considerations were involved in the founding of Copenhagen and Uppsala in Scandinavia, and St. Andrews, Glasgow, and Aberdeen in Scotland. Typical was the case of Prague, which was a project of Charles IV, King of Bohemia, with the full cooperation of the Papacy. There was an obvious effort here to make Prague the metropolis of the Holy Roman Empire, to provide a center for Bohemia's intellectuals, and to strengthen the kingdom by attracting scholars from the outside. The university "was a highly conscious, politically motivated foundation, totally lacking in those features of slower academic growth which had characterized many of the earlier *studia* in western Europe."[28]

In any case, the university as an instrument for the organization of higher learning, had obviously come to stay. By the end of the fifteenth century there were at least seventy-nine universities in Europe. Henceforth, the university would be the dominant and unchallenged institution of higher education for the entire Western world and, later, for the rest of the globe as well.

Organization and Government of the Medieval University

As the medieval universities achieved a fuller and more highly defined structure, they customarily came to have four distinct subdivisions or "faculties": arts, law, medicine, and theology. The last three were considered higher or "superior" faculties for which, presumably, the arts course was preparatory. The masters, who were duly admitted members of each faculty, elected their own proctor or dean. Usually the four deans then selected a rector to represent the entire university, but it did not always work out that way. At Paris, the rector was originally merely the head of the arts faculty, and it took some doing to gain recognition for him as head of the entire university. "It was not till after a long series of struggles," Rashdall observes, "that the Rector fought his way to the headship of the university, and the fighting was very literal fighting; on several occasions it assumed the form of a physical encounter in church between the partisans of the Rector and those of the Dean of Theology."[29]

As the scholars of the university faculties became more organized, they also became more obviously professional. One sign of this was the new economics of instruction. Previously, the masters had been somewhat haphazard in the fees that they charged for their services. Some, notably the monastic teachers of the early middle ages, had dispensed instruction *gratis*. But in the thirteenth century, the business of higher education became highly competitive and the supply of adequate church benefices or endowments was in increasingly short supply. As a result, the masters began to charge set fees for their instruction.[30]

To have a voice in the affairs of a master's university or guild, one first had to be accepted as a member of the same; this meant, in essence, that one had been approved as a teaching professional. All medieval degrees were in their inception teaching degrees. Master, doctor, and professor "meant one and the same thing—teacher," Morison reminds us. "Admission to the degree meant that you belonged to the guild of teachers, and began at once to teach the subjects you had just learned."[31] Every faculty, by the way, had its own master's degree, but the masters in the higher, or professional, faculties such as law, medicine, and theology, came in time to be called *doctores* or *professores*.

Curriculum. The first formal stage of instruction in a medieval university was a general arts course leading to a ceremony (or debate) known as "determination," which was the equivalent of a bachelor's degree. After two more years of study under a master, the young man was eligible for recognition as a candidate for the master's degree or license itself. At this point the aspiring bachelor was formally invested as a "licentiate." There followed another period of study and lecturing, during which the candidate hoped by some master work or other achievement to demonstrate that he should be admitted into the master's guild. Once accepted, he was formally recognized as a fellow master at an imposing ceremony known as "inception." If the aspiring student wished to study theology, medicine, or law, he first had to be accepted as Master of Arts. He would then be eligible to study in one of the higher faculties.[32]

Today it is assumed that the medieval university's curriculum was strongly theological. To be sure, the dominant study in thirteenth-century Paris was theology, but this was not typical. It is surprising to discover how frankly utilitarian the medieval curriculum was. In most universities theology was the least popular subject and attracted the fewest students mainly because it was thought to be too theoretical. Among the higher faculties, civil law was usually the most popular field, with canon law a close second, and then medicine. Harry Elmer Barnes characterizes the medieval universities as "corporations whose industries were teaching and learning." They were in business primarily to train civil and ecclesiastical administrators, lawyers, and medical doctors, not philosophers, pure scientists, or literary scholars.[33]

The available evidence suggests that Louis Paetow is correct when he asserts that the medieval universities were an obstacle to the study of the classics. Paetow argues that the universities actually delayed the coming of the humanistic renaissance until the late fourteenth and fifteenth centuries, that classical studies "were smothered by the universities with their emphasis on logic, law, medicine, and theology." The medieval arts course, from a present-day perspective, appears narrow and specialized. Not only were most of the ancient classics omitted, but there was also "an entire lack of experimental sciences, of modern languages as well as history and the other so-called social sciences."[34]

Although hindsight might lead us to characterize these conditions as deficiencies, the clients of the medieval university seemed to be satisfied with its offerings. Its classrooms were usually well-filled, for the institution was one of the few mechanisms of upward mobility in the middle ages, and its utilitarian curriculum was thought to pave the way for a successful career. As Rashdall puts it, "to the ambitious youth of the thirteenth century whose soul rebelled against the narrow limits of his native manor, his native farm, or his native shop, . . . the university offered a real chance for escape. To the boy conscious only of brains and energy the universities brought all the glittering prizes of the Church within the limits of practicable ambition." And he adds: "In the north of Europe, the Church was simply a synonym for the professions."[35]

Not only was much of the training in the "higher" faculties frankly vocational, but the medieval university for a time included what we would call today a business course or, more properly, a program in secretarial science. This was the course in the *ars dictaminis* (the art of letter-writing) sometimes called the *ars notaria* (the notary art). There was a great need for men trained in the art of preparing correspondence, executing legal documents, and drawing up proclamations and other types of state papers. These studies were developed as a practical branch of the medieval rhetorical course. They flourished from the twelfth to the fourteenth centuries in universities, such as Bologna, that featured legal training as a specialty.[36]

Methods of Instruction. The principal methods of instruction that prevailed in the medieval university were the *lectio* (lecture) and the *quaestiones disputatae* (disputation). The *lectio* consisted of the master reading the texts of certain classic authors to his class and making comments (glosses) on these works. Such lecture courses were based entirely on specified books. Many historians have argued that lecturing predominated as the accepted mode of instruction in the medieval period because there was as yet no printing press and books were scarce. Samuel Morison disputes this, however, and points out that medieval students could rent books cheaply from *scriptoria* where nonilluminated manuscripts were prepared in large quantities. Whatever the situation, lecturing went on at such a clip that young candidates for the master of arts degree were expected to prepare themselves for that honor by lecturing, *docendo discere* (learn to teach by teaching). In practice, this meant assisting the regular masters by giving "extraordinary" lectures to help beginning students or substituting for professors who were away on ecclesiastical or political missions. The very title "doctor," as it pertained to members of the three higher faculties, meant teacher, since it was derived from the Latin verb *docere,* to teach.[37]

The agelong battle of wits between professor and class had its uniquely medieval aspects. Because the teaching masters were not paid regular salaries and had to rely on student fees to eke out a precarious living, it was alleged from time to time that they resorted to cheap tricks and attention-getting appeals in order to attract a large audience. In turn, students were said to have whistled, hissed, shouted, groaned, shuffled their feet, and even thrown stones at lecturers who were inaudible, who spoke too slowly to cover the material fully, or who lectured too fast for the students to take full notes.[38]

Despite the ever-present lecturing, medieval higher education was not merely passive; it had a strong element of argumentativeness due to the disputation and its *pro et contra* technique. The disputation gave the medieval student a rare opportunity to express himself and perform in public in an oral debate wherein a student or master sought to maintain a proposition against another student or master. Abelard had pioneered in using this method with his famous work *Sic et Non* (Yes and Its Opposite). The argument was supposed to follow faithfully the rules of logic incorporated in Aristotle's work, *Organon.* In other words, the *thesis* or *quaestio* (question) was to be explored by means of presenting a major premise and one or more minor premises, followed by a syllogism, statement of fallacies, and refutation of the opposing arguments. The Church valued the scholastic disputation highly, believing it to be the best means of repelling heresy with supposedly irrefutable logic.[39]

At the University of Paris in the thirteenth century disputed questions were proposed by the master every two weeks as a class exercise. The master attempted to resolve these issues, or as it was then stated, to "deter-mine" them, by judging the merits of the students' various arguments and the validity of their proofs. Twice a year, at Christmas and Easter, the masters themselves held great debates before large audiences of students. These were the disputations of *quaestiones quodlibetales* (whatsoever you will).[40]

Most universities followed standardized procedures for disputation that had been set up at the University of Paris. "From the time he ceased to be a freshman," Mori-son observes, "the medieval student was constantly prac-ticing this art, and at every important stage of his academic career he had to take part in public disputations, either as respondent or opponent. . . ."[41] As a result, the atmosphere of the medieval university was dynamic and lively, full of argumentativeness and disputatious at-titude. But like the *ars dictaminis*, the disputation had a utilitarian purpose. It undoubtedly served to sharpen the skills of the professional men who in later life would have to dispute in law courts, in feudal assemblies, and in eccle-siastical convocations. Meanwhile, Huizinga writes, dur-ing their university days, "collision and struggle of opin-ions and parties" frequently dominated the scene. There were "frequent elections and rowdyism of the stu-dents. . . . quarrels of all sorts of orders, schools, and groups. The different colleges contended among them-selves, the secular clergy were at variance with the regu-lar."[42]

The Rise of Colleges

In the medieval universities, colleges made their first appearance as privately endowed charitable foundations serving as hostels or residences for needy students. Such was the Collège de Dix-Huit in Paris, founded about 1180, which may very well have been the first college. Many more followed in Paris and elsewhere. The arts students in the medieval university were usually younger than the regular law or theology scholars. The university authorities feared that these lads would be victimized by the townspeople and might be more prone to riot than the mature students. The college residence provided a secure refuge or hospice, much like a monstery, under the charge of a master. In time, this came to be a rigidly supervised environment where strict discipline was enforced and the students were locked inside the college gates at night.[43]

The colleges multiplied rapidly in France, England, and other countries, and eventually the resident masters began to add tutorial duties to their supervisory functions. Students in the colleges were offered "extraordinary" lectures (supplemental or review lectures), taught either by regular professors or by resident assistant masters. As these educational activities increased, the colleges came practically to monopolize the teaching of the liberal arts in certain universities. In Paris, for example, first the faculty of theology—and later the whole university—came to be identified with the college founded in 1257 by Robert de Sorbon and originally designed for graduate masters of arts who were studying theology. By the fifteenth century, some of the colleges had grown very rich through real-estate operations. "Like some of the monasteries," Ben-David notes, "they became seigneuries ruled by small oligarchies, and these oligarchies dominated the whole university." Some of them had become "institutions that catered to the sons of the privileged classes rather than to the international community of scholars."[44]

On the European continent the colleges eventually were absorbed by the universities or, as in France, were swept away by the revolution of 1789. Only one continental college still survives: the Collegio di Spagna at the University of Bologna.[45] In England, however, the reverse occurred. The colleges not only survived, they became teaching institutions, and as such came to rule the universities.

The first English college, Merton, was founded at Oxford in 1274 by Walter de Merton. A number of other collegiate foundations followed at both Oxford and Cambridge. An important step was taken when William of Wykeham in the late fourteenth century ordered that special payments be made by his foundation—New College, Oxford—to those Senior Fellows who were engaged in teaching the younger Fellows. Most of the other English colleges followed suit, and the result was that by the sixteenth century these institutions had become virtually autonomous. By that time the lectures and tutorials given in the colleges had almost totally superseded lectures given by the English universities as such. The colleges were now providing an almost complete curriculum.[46]

Significance of the Medieval University

The medieval university differed in a number of significant ways from its modern counterpart. The physical facilities available to students were at best minimal compared with the relatively sumptuous ones characteristic of many modern institutions. There were, furthermore, no formal entrance requirements, in contrast to present-day schools. Students freely moved from university to university. Language was no barrier. "Latin was the language of instruction from St. Andrews to Salerno, and from Cracow to Coimbra."[47]

There were, moreover, no mass enrollments at the medieval university. Unlike the university of our day, the

medieval university served the needs of only a tiny seg-
ment of the population. A study of fourteenth-century
Oxford shows that the feudality (the political leadership of
that time) had little if any need for the training that the
university then offered.[48] J. W. Adamson observed that the
medieval university "did not include a very powerful body
of persons, women as well as men. The men of action, the
soldier, the great landowner, the sovereign prince, and
their respective women-folk received little or no help from
. . . universities."[49]

There was, of course, little if any provision for the
university education of women in the middle ages; higher
education would remain an exclusively male prerogative
for many centuries. Nevertheless, it is remarkable that a
few talented women obtained the opportunity to pursue
higher studies at Bologna. In the thirteenth century,
Novella and Bettina Calderini, whose parents both held
doctorates, were students at the university there. Indeed,
when their father or their husbands were obliged to be
absent from their teaching duties, it is reported that these
young ladies substituted on the lecture platform. Novella
was said to have been so beautiful that she was compelled
to veil her face so that she would not distract her hearers.
This tradition of "women's liberation" at the University of
Bologna continued into the seventeenth and eighteenth
centuries, when talented women scientists such as Laura
Bassi and Anna Morandi lectured there.[50]

In public affairs the medieval university played a role
that was at least as significant as that of modern institutions of learning. In some respects, the medieval institution was even more influential. Along with the Holy Roman Empire and the Papacy, the universities of the middle
ages constituted an international tribunal of sorts. In the
late fourteenth century, for example, the University of
Paris led the way in a campaign to end the Great Schism

which was dividing the Papacy at the time. University representatives toured Europe to drum up support for a great church council to end this ecclesiastical split, and when the Council of Constance was at last convened, the universities of Europe had an important part in its proceedings.[51]

How much intellectual freedom was there at the medieval university? In the early days, apparently a surprising amount. There were few recorded instances in the twelfth and thirteenth centuries of actual repression; persecution of dissenters and heretics seems to have emerged only in later years—during the fourteenth and fifteenth centuries.[52] Attempts by the authorities to suppress discussion of new ideas at the universities often proved unavailing. A good example was the effort at Paris in 1210 to ban all reading or teaching of Aristotle's newly recovered philosophical and scientific writings. By 1255 this prohibition had become so ineffective that these books were not only being studied in Paris's faculty of arts, but were, in fact, prescribed reading. Probably the reason for this bold and independent attitude in the early days of the medieval university was its shifting and transient international clientele plus the fact that it was substantially unhampered by property holdings: it could always proclaim *cessatio*, pull up stakes, and leave if any attempt were made to infringe upon its academic autonomy.

In the early days the medieval universities may well have been exciting centers of learning. Robert Grosseteste, the first chancellor of Oxford University, was interested in a wide range of subjects, including medicine, astronomy, philosophy, the calendar, and the magnifying properties of lenses. One of his students was the scientist Roger Bacon.[53] Medieval scholars in their disputations and investigations were, after all, proceeding on the assumption that the nature of God and of the cosmos itself could be examined by man rationally and critically.[54]

The medieval university in perspective merits a high rank in the history of Western culture. Many characteristics of our present-day universities derive ultimately from these typically medieval institutions. As Hastings Rashdall observes, ". . . in the form in which we have them, teaching corporations, courses of study, examinations, degrees, [all] are a direct inheritance from the Middle Ages."[55]

2

The Renaissance

L'art pour l'art!—that was the watchword of the Renaissance humanists. But this ideal was not easily realized in the universities of their day, for those institutions primarily served as training schools for prospective clergymen, physicians, government administrators, and lawyers. As such, they could hardly make the pursuit of belles lettres, history, poetry, and art *for its own sake* their primary goal. If the Renaissance humanists hoped to cultivate such "pure" learning, they had to do it outside the university's gates. This, however, is not surprising. Even today, the university in many ways is a remarkably conservative institution. The situation was not very different in the fifteenth and sixteenth centuries.

Must we assume, then, that the classical Renaissance had little to do with higher education? Not necessarily. To determine the interrelations, if any, between universities and Renaissance humanism, it is necessary to review specific events in particular countries. A good place to begin is Italy, where the Renaissance reached its peak in the fifteenth century. And historians agree that it would be difficult to find a more thriving center of Renaissance culture than the city of Florence.

After research in the Florentine archives, a modern scholar states: "Intellectual activity in medieval and Renaissance Florence was predominantly—almost exclusively—functional; it was related to specific vocational and professional purposes. . . . The educational system was organized to train some boys for mercantile careers and others for professional careers in law, the notarial discipline, medicine, and theology."[1] A survey of Florentine public pronouncements and enactments dealing with higher education bears out the truth of this statement. Neither the general public nor the city's leadership was especially committed to humanist learning at the university. In fact, the characteristic humanist studies—those which examined the condition, heritage, achievements, and prospects of man—flourished best *outside* the local university in places such as Marsilio Ficino's Platonic Academy.[2] The university, on the other hand, featured traditional metaphysical, theological, legal, and medical studies. Moreover, support for even these established fields was somewhat uncertain. The University of Florence was actually a publicly supported institution, and public moneys, when given at all, tended to be dispensed most grudgingly. In 1413, its budget was cut drastically, Moreover, the university appropriation was repeatedly trimmed in the years that followed. This state of affairs, however, did not trouble many wealthy and influential Florentines; they usually sent their sons to schools such as Bologna or Padua. Meanwhile local politicians questioned the wisdom of making any appropriations for the university. One of the most influential of them, Rinaldo degli Albizzi, said that it would be better to spend the money on the city's military needs.[3]

The attitude of the skeptical city fathers was hardly

improved by reports of alleged misconduct on the part of university professors. Take for example the information the councillors received in 1398 about the university's rector, an enterprising fellow named Dino of Lucca. It seems that Dino, to make sure that he would be reappointed to this important post, ordered the professors to stop lecturing and closed the school's doors. Then he hid the keys in order to prevent the students from meeting to elect a new rector! Not surprisingly, the Board of Governors launched an investigation into Dino's regime, and soon found out that he had imposed fines upon students without seeming justification and later used this money "to entertain several scholars, who were his henchmen, in his house, in which he permitted gambling and other dishonest activities. . . ."[4]

Nor was this all. Earlier complaints reached the Florentine government about the alleged defects of the university. As far back as September 1366, the councillors were told that "professors omit much material which they are required to cover according to the customs of the Studio [school]." Two years later, a disgruntled student presented a complaint alleging that the professors at Florence did not cover the scheduled course material and failed to hold promised disputations. Some only had one or two students. According to the complainant, the professors with their big salaries were robbing "this commune as boldly as if they were highwaymen." The student concluded: "Send for them and learn how they teach. Their evil habits are so numerous that I cannot describe them all to you!"[5] One can well imagine the impression that complaints of this kind made on city councillors, many of whom as guildsmen or town artisans had little hope of ever being able to send their own sons to the university.

The humanist contribution to the university's enterprise as a whole remained for a long time rather minimal.

In Florence, as elsewhere, university humanism was at first mainly an extracurricular activity. From time to time a famous literary scholar or a learned Greek savant might be appointed to a university lectureship, but most public support was reserved for professional education. Even at the height of the renowned Medicean hegemony in the city, the arts and humanities faculty remained small in comparison with the more specifically vocational ones. The bulk of the university's budget went for legal and medical education. The few professors in arts and letters were the most poorly paid of any at the university.[6]

In fifteenth-century Italy there were, of course, universities that were better endowed, better attended, and better regarded by the public than Florence's. But even in these schools, the primary emphasis was vocational, not humanist. Bologna, for example, was widely known for legal training, while Padua was equally famous for its medical school.[7] Even in the Renaissance arts curriculum there was no sharp break with the past. Paul Kristeller has shown that Aristotelian philosophy, which had become the main support of medieval scholasticism, continued to thrive at the Renaissance universities. There were new interpretations of it, to be sure, as some scholars sought to recover the "true" Aristotle and to add Platonic or humanist elements to its exposition.[8]

North of the Alps many of the same phenomena were present. As in Italy, universities continued to emphasize Aristotelian philosophy in the traditional training for the clergy. As in Italy, they stressed professional training for law and medicine while viewing the arts course as preparatory or incidental. In some universities, however, the initial response to humanism was more hostile than in others. At the University of Paris, for example, many scholastics on the faculty were positively vehement in their opposition to "the New Learning." Italian humanists

in turn spoke with contempt of these "northern barbarians": *Nullus doctus in Gallia*. [There are no true teachers
in Gaul] Erasmus of Rotterdam, bored by the old books of
scholastic philosophy he found at the Sorbonne in 1497,
could scarcely stay awake as he listened to the learned
Magistri Nostri, "those holy Scotists," with their "wrinkled
brows, staring eyes, and puzzled faces." The disgusted
Dutch humanist told a young English friend that "nothing
is more rotten than their brains, nothing more barbarous
than their language, nothing duller than their interests,
nothing thornier than their learning, nothing rougher
than their manners, nothing more hypocritical than their
lives, more venomous than their speech or blacker than
their hearts."[9] Other humanists were equally exasperated
with the "old guard" on the Paris faculty. Philip Melanchthon, a German humanist, aimed his fire at John Major,
one of the most prominent of traditionalists: "Good
heavens! What wagon loads of trifling! What pages he fills
with disputes, whether there can be horsiness without a
horse, and whether the sea was salt when God made it."
Major was also reported to have discussed, perhaps as a
philosophical exercise, whether God could become an ox,
an ass, or a gourd, if He so desired, and whether John the
Baptist's head, when cut off, could have been in more
than one place at a time.[10] However, these are rather extreme examples of scholastic sophistry and probably are
not representative of the best philosophy instruction at
Paris.

In Germany we find that humanism *at first* encountered suspicion and hostility from university professors
and met with disinterest or even derision on the part of
the students. It was something new, unfamiliar, impracti-
cal. Scholasticism was well entrenched; professional
preparation was the chief concern of higher education. On
top of this, the "New Learning" seemed to many Germans

to be a subversive foreign importation, coming as it did from much-hated Italy. For these reasons, some German universities reacted bitterly to the new studies. At the University of Leipsig, for example, a salaried lecturer on the classics and the humanities, Johannes Rhagius Aesticampianus, was forced to resign. His parting thrust at his critics, delivered in the form of a farewell oration in September 1511, cursed roundly all "those who have pursued me with hate and jealousy, who have envied my position, who have never dined or even talked with me, who have closed off their lecture halls, who have kept their students away from my lectures and have otherwise criticized their value."[11] One cannot help but wonder if such anti-humanist furor was due at least as much to secret fears of losing enrollment in traditional university programs as it was to anxiety that the new studies would undermine piety, orthodoxy, and morality among the students.

Though acrimony often leads to exaggeration among disputants, it is reasonable to assume from the number of cases and the bitterness engendered that some humanists were actually a bit *too* "human" to fulfill traditional academic functions. German detractors of humanism sought to inhibit its growth by any means their lively imaginations could conceive. Thus, at the University of Ingolstadt a humanist professor, Conrad Celtis, was denounced by colleagues and students for his casual approach to professional duties. His students even sent him a formal complaint in 1496 stating: "You accuse us of madness and charge that we are stupid barbarians, and you call wild beasts those whose fees support you. . . . This we might have borne with better grace but for the fact that you yourself abound in the faults of which you accuse us. For what of the fact that while you carp about us, you yourself are so torpid from dissipation that in conversation your drowsy head drops to your elbow like a figure eight?" Another humanist of questionable character was Peter Luder, who taught the Latin classics at Heidelberg. He had such a reputation for heavy drinking and womanizing that many parents refused to send their sons to his classes. And Jacob Locher's dismissal from the University of Freiburg may have been due more to his "obstreperous" life-style than to his humanist teachings.[12] While such cases were probably more the exception than the rule, it is clear that humanism in some Renaissance universities encountered opposition on personal as well as intellectual grounds.

Conservative members of the European university community saw the humanistic Renaissance as threatening vested academic interests, undermining the professional mission of the university, and possibly even subverting the faith that higher learning had always pledged itself to uphold. Moreover, they were suspicious of the humanists' trilingual approach to language and literature instruction. Medieval Latin, especially as incorporated in the much revered Vulgate text of the Holy Scriptures, was a symbol to them of orthodoxy, true wisdom, and sound learning. Greek, on the other hand, bore strong overtones, in their eyes, of heresy, schism, and possibly even paganism, while Hebrew was suspect as the tongue of the "despised unbelieving" Jews. Thus what the humanists proudly proposed as a major educational advance appeared to the upholders of the status quo to be an irresponsible and subversive attack on the principles of true learning. These fears proved to be excessive; the Renaissance did not really revolutionize the university. The traditional organization of faculties remained the same as in the Middle Ages as did the system of academic government. Nevertheless, there were some changes in higher education during these years that can be linked to the Renaissance. We see them most clearly in the evolution of the university curriculum, particularly the curriculum of the arts faculties. A number of the newer human-centered studies of the Renaissance, such as Greek literature, rhetoric, poetry, history, and Platonic philosophy, eventually took their place alongside the older scholastic courses. The former remained tangential and elective compared with the professional courses, to be sure, but at least they now had a secure and recognized niche.

How did these curricular changes come about? The circumstances, not surprisingly, varied from country to country. In Italy, both native and foreign teachers played a significant role in promoting the study of *bonae litterae*. Most active among the foreigners was a group of visiting Greeks, many of them refugees from their homeland, which was coming under the control of the Turks. Displaced Greek scholars such as John Argyropoulos, Andromicus Callixtus, Demetrius Chalcondylas, and John Lascaris were seeking academic employment and were happy to find it at the Italian universities. They lectured on the language and literature of ancient Greece and in the process stirred up a considerable enthusiasm for Greek studies among Italian students. Witness, for example, the excitement of a young student at the University of Perugia who reported on the lectures by Chalcondylas: "A Greek has just come, and has begun to teach me with great diligence, while I listen to him with indescribable pleasure, because he is a Greek. . . . It seems to me, as if in him were mirrored the wisdom, the refined intelligence, and the elegance of those famous men of old."[13]

Italian scholars carried forward with great success the work that the Greeks had started. Such talented teachers as Guarino da Verona achieved fame as specialists on the classics. Guarino had studied in Constantinople and later became a professor of Greek at the University of Ferrara. In the middle of the fifteenth century it was reported that people came to study with him from far off England, France, Germany, and Hungary, as well as from all over Italy. With some exaggeration, perhaps, it was said that students would gather in great numbers on the coldest winter days outside the unopened doors of his lecture room, waiting for him to appear. In the same way, Francesco Filelfo was building a notable reputation as a classicist while teaching at the universities of Venice, Bologna, and Florence. This zealous humanist reputedly brought back from Constantinople a veritable treasure trove of classical manuscripts. His aim was to give no fewer than four lectures a day: Cicero and Homer in the morning, Terence and Thucydides in the afternoon. Like Guarino, he was said to have attracted students from all over Europe. A third great Italian exponent of the "New Learning," Angelo Ambrogini (called Poliziano after his birthplace) appeared on the scene a little later. As professor of Greek and Latin at Florence, Poliziano was acclaimed for his high standards of scholarship and his devastating attacks on Ciceronian formalism. He also was a brilliant rhetorician who sometimes began a lecture course with a long original poem to set the mood for the literary analysis that was to follow. At some Italian universities, students were inspired by lectures such as these to write their own satiric comedies in Latin, frequently modeled on Plautus. These works (definitely extracurricular!) were sometimes performed by student actors at carnival time just before the coming of spring or they might be given on the eve of doctoral examinations.[14]

The teachings of a Chalcondylas, a Filelfo, or a Poliziano probably only had a minimal impact on the professional schools, but students in the arts courses were attracted to them. As a matter of fact, humanism made the most headway in the *newer* Italian universities, such as those at Pavia, Ferrara, Pisa, and Rome. There, a sort of academic compromise was worked out between the old and the new. Roberto Weiss puts it well when he writes: "The simultaneous presence of medieval and new elements, so noticeable in school teaching, was also to be found at the universities. . . . Side-by-side with a good deal of traditional learning, one could also find at the universities the new values of humanism. . . . What actually happened . . . was a working compromise, by which the old and new traditions were able to work together in harmony for a long time and without too much rivalry."[15]

Even so, the most flourishing centers of Italian humanism were to be found in the academies, not the universities. Academies were private or quasi-private institutions organized to give humanists a public forum and a rallying point. These centers developed all across the peninsula—in Florence, Venice, Ferrara, Mantua, Milan, Rome, and Naples. Such gathering places of like-minded intellectuals had no set schedules for classes, or lectures. They met in various private residences from time to time, such as Lorenzo de Medici's Florentine palace or his villa at Fiesole. The best-known organization of this type, the Platonic Academy of Florence, had a select membership composed of literary scholars, poets, philosophers, and aristocratic culture-seekers. During their meetings these initiates might study a Platonic dialogue, criticize other Greek or Latin texts, or speculate about the meaning of life (what, they might debate, is *virtú*, or *fama*, or *fortunà*)? The closest the group ever came to holding a formally scheduled session was its annual *convivium* on the seventh of November. This gathering was in honor of Plato, and it was always held in front of a bust of the famed philosopher. Flowers decorated the statue and a lamp burned solemnly before it.[16]

In France, it will be recalled, humanism had to fight for its life in the face of the unremitting hostility of many of the learned doctors of the Sorbonne. But its prospects began to improve when the king came to its aid. The energetic humanist-scholar Guillaume Budé was able to persuade King Francis I that it would be a splendid idea to establish a new institution of learning in Paris primarily for humanist studies. This royal foundation, the Collège de France, gave an enthusiastic welcome to the new classical learning and to all studies centering on man. In 1530, a number of special chairs were created in this "warming hearth of Fench humanism" for professors of Greek, Latin, Hebrew, French, and Philosophy. In this way the antagonistic scholastics of the Sorbonne were bypassed. In addition, French municipal governments at Bordeaux, Lyons, Orléans, Rheims, and Montpellier founded local institutions of higher learning that were similarly hospitable to humanist teachings."[17] Again, as in Italy, it was mainly the newer, less hidebound institutions that were willing to introduce the new studies.

Previous to this time, a few adventurous humanists had even tried to "bore from within" at the sometimes skeptical, frequently hostile University of Paris. One of the boldest of these was a wandering Italian, the "clever, pushing, loose-principled, and frivolous" Fausto Andrelini, who became a close friend of Desiderius Erasmus. Andrelini succeeded in giving university lectures at Paris on the classical poets. These lectures proved to be eminently successful. Another local recruit to the humanist cause from the enemy camp was Robert Gaguin, literary scholar, historian, and professor at the University of Paris. The three—Andrelini, Gaguin, and Erasmus—became fast friends. Often they dined together at Gaguin's apartments. On one such occasion, the host greeted his companions with an epigram[18]:

Welcome, O Faustus, bard loved by Apollo;
Welcome no less, Erasmus, who dost follow

As Faustus' comrade. Not with flowing cup
I greet you; meagerly must poets sup.

Humanism soon spread north from France to the universities of the Lowlands. The University of Leyden won the reputation of being one of the principal centers in all Europe of the "New Learning," and the humanist program at the University of Louvain flourished impressively. Louvain's Collegium Trilingue attracted students from countries far and near who came to pursue literary studies in Greek and Hebrew as well as Latin.[19]

In Germany, "humane letters" made more rapid headway after 1500 then before, perhaps because the new studies came to be linked in the public mind with the cause of ecclesiastical reformation. In this connection it should be remembered that some of the most prominent German humanists—university professors like Philip Melanchthon—played an active part in the Lutheran Reformation.

Whatever the reasons, the evidence is clear that humanist teachings were acquiring a wider audience in German universities in the sixteenth century. More and more expounders of the new studies were being appointed to university professorships. The number of course offerings in humanist subjects such as Greek, Hebrew, poetry, oratory, history, and Latin literature was increasing. Some younger faculty members now felt emboldened to predict that "the new studies would bring about a spiritual as well as a cultural reform" in Germany. Conrad Mutian wrote exultantly from Erfurt that "more and more young masters are deserting scholasticism for the study of good letters." Also the humanists now felt strong enough to launch a counterattack on their traditionalist opponents, heaping scorn on scholastic methods of teaching in the widely disseminated tract, *Epistolae Obscurorum Virorum* [Letters of Obscure Men]. The upshot of all of this was that humanist studies became an accepted part of the arts course at leading German universities, including Erfurt, Wittenberg, Heidelberg, Nuremberg, Vienna, and Basel. At Cologne and Freiburg, however, the scholastics remained more influential and held out for a long time against the new wave.[20]

In England the new humane learning began to attract a select group of devotees in the last two decades of the fifteenth century. One of the most assiduous, William Grocyn, had studied in Italy with renowned humanists. As early as 1490, Grocyn was lecturing on the ancient Greek language and literature at Oxford. A physician, Thomas Linacre, worked closely with him to establish Oxonian classical studies on a firm footing. The next generation of prominent English humanists, represented by such able scholars as John Colet, Thomas More, William Lilly, and Bishop John Fisher, secured an even wider recognition in London and in the universities during the early sixteenth century. Bishop Fisher, when elected Chancellor of Cambridge University, took advantage of his strategic position to work for the establishment of a new kind of college that would feature the "New Learning" as the core of its curriculum. This school, St. Johns, made its debut in 1511 and provided ample opportunities for instruction in Greek and Hebrew. It was Fisher, too, who was responsible primarily for the invitation to the most famous humanist in the world, Desiderius Erasmus, to come to Cambridge and teach Greek. In 1540 the final triumph of humanism in England was assured by the crown itself. In that year King Henry VIII founded the Regius Professorships at Oxford and Cambridge for instruction in "Divinity, Civil Law, Physic, Hebrew and Greek."[21] Thus, over a span of three generations the learning of the humanists steadily expanded its influence in England until it was established solidly in the country's citadels of higher learning and among important members of the power elite.

Why had English humanism triumphed so signally? For one thing, it should be recalled the English people were undergoing a profound religious and political revolution at this time. This was the age of the English Reformation and the confiscation of monastic wealth. Under the circumstances, it was natural that the Tudor sovereigns, Henry VIII and Elizabeth I, should look with suspicion on the old "monkish" and scholastic learning as somehow connected with "Papist" opposition to their rule. Accordingly, the very considerable influence of these absolute monarchs was employed in favor of the new, "reformed" learning. At the same time, the study of humane letters came to be identified in England with a life of action and with preparation for a career of practical achievement. This differed somewhat from its more abstract role on the Continent. As Douglas Bush puts it, "English humanism wished to produce citizens and statesmen, not scholars."[22]

The consequences of the new situation were soon apparent in the universities. In earlier times, Oxford and Cambridge had been essentially training schools for *clerici*—acolytes and priests, novices and monks. In the sixteenth century, however, these schools were being inundated by large numbers of laymen who contemplated an active secular career. These young people (and their parents, too) regarded the newly fashionable study of humane letters as a passport to the much-desired honorific status of gentleman. An Anglican clergyman realistically assessed the motivations that now predominated even among clerical students when he remarked: "If any man could understand Greek, there was a Deanery for him; if Latin, a good living." And Richard Mulcaster observed that now "everyone desireth to have his children acquire learning." The inevitable result of this

pragmatic concern was a sizable increase in university enrollments. By the middle of the sixteenth century, Oxford
and Cambridge were crowded with students from upper-
middle-class homes who aspired to a university training.
Many of these gentlemen had little, if any, serious interest
in "polite learning" for its own sake; they hoped, however, that its acquisition, no matter how superficial, might
further their social and vocational ambitions. William
Latimer saw the way things were going. "There be none
now but great men's sons in Colleges," he complained,
"and their fathers look not to have them preachers." And
the playwright Thomas Nashe, contemplating the same
scene, concluded: "Pride the perverter of all Vertue, sit-
teth appareled in the Marchants Spoiles, . . . and scorneth
learning, that gave their upstart Father, titles of gentry."[23]

With such powerful social forces abroad in the land,
the scholastic opponents of the new teachings could fight
only a rearguard action. When Corpus Christi College was
founded at Oxford in 1516 and gained the reputation of
being a center of humanist studies, students from the
other colleges, perhaps encouraged by their professors,
formed gangs of "Trojans," which proceeded to assault
the inoffensive "Greeks" from the new institution. But this
was soon stopped by King Henry VIII, who quickly dispatched a letter to Oxford commanding that all such in-
timidation of the Greek scholars cease. About this time,
too, Thomas More, who was later to be a close confidant of
the king, castigated those Oxford dons who still distrusted
having Greek instruction at the university: "This fellow
declares that only theology should be studied; but if he
admits even that, I don't see how he can accomplish his
aim without some knowledge of languages, whether Hebrew or Greek or Latin."[24]

The English opponents of humanism fought a losing
battle as the century wore on, but they fought bitterly.
William Tyndale, some years later, recalled

. . . the old barking curs, Duns' disciples and like draff called Scotists, the children of darkness, raged in every pulpit against Greek, Latin and Hebrew, some beating the pulpit with their fists for madness, and roaring with open and foaming mouth that if there were but one Terence or Virgil in the world, and that same in their sleeves, and a fire before them, they would burn them therein, though it should cost them their lives.[25]

Classical and humanist-oriented studies in England received a significant boost from 1510 to 1513 when Erasmus of Rotterdam taught Greek at Cambridge. "Tradition sees him," writes Margaret Phillips, "pacing the riverside walk opposite the old red-brick front of Queens'. . . . Not far from Queens' . . . was the mighty chapel of King's which had been building for over sixty years. . . . The actual fabric . . . was completed in 1515, and Erasmus may well, on his after-dinner walks, have watched the masons putting the final touches to the intricate stonework."[26] Not surprisingly, the visiting celebrity received what he considered to be unfair criticism from opponents of humanism at the university, but he remained proud of his accomplishments there. Reflecting on his career at Cambridge some years later, he claimed: "Now the university is so flourishing, that it can compete with the best universities of the age. It contains men, compared with whom theologians of the old school seem only the ghosts of theologians."

One of these scholars of the new school, quite possibly inspired by the example set by Erasmus, was John Cheke of St. Johns College, who in 1540 was appointed the Regius Professor of Greek. A colleague reported that the students were making excellent progress under Cheke's tutelage. Many of them were reading Aristotle and Plato in the original Greek, according to this account. Nor was this all; "Sophocles and Euripides are more famil-

iar authors than Plautus was in your time," reported this
scholar. "Herodotus, Thucydides, and Xenophon are
more conned and discussed than Livy was then. De-
mosthenes is as familiar an author as Cicero used to be;
and there are more copies of Isocrates in use than there
formerly were of Terence. Nor do we disregard the Latin
authors, but study with the greatest zeal the choicest
writers of the best period."[27]

What was the overall impact of the Renaissance on
the university? As has been noted, neither the institutional structure nor the societal functions of the university
were changed radically by the Renaissance humanists. On
the other hand, changes did occur in the curriculum of arts
faculties from Italy to England. But how significant were
these changes? Did they give rise to an intellectual revolution? The answer depends to some extent on a matter of
definition. Arnold Toynbee, for his part, is skeptical of the
achievements of the Renaissance and sees it as merely
abrogating "the intellectual authority of the Christian religion in favour of that of the Greek and Latin classics." He
holds that, intellectually speaking, the progress of Western man has been due not to humanistic studies but to the
development of a spirit of critical inquiry and its eventual
application to science and technology.[28]

Admittedly, the Renaissance university contributed
little to scientific learning.[29] Toynbee, however, ignores
the fact that by turning to the classics the Renaissance
humanists were utilizing a freer, less catechistic type of
learning. The *studia humanitatis* were concerned above all
with man and his potential for growth. Having abrogated
the authority of rigid scholasticism, they were able to
serve meaningfully the personal and cultural needs of sixteenth century students. For that time they *were* the new,
innovative, liberating studies—"the New Learning." And
in our own time when universities seek to establish a gen-

eral education core that will lend unity to the many specialized curriculums and serve human needs as a whole, they are in essence following the path first blazed by the Renaissance humanists.

In the long run, the Renaissance humanists contributed an important new spirit to higher education, a liberal spirit in the sense that it was "liberating." Wilhelm Windelband saw this when he wrote: "One could almost feel the impulsive blood of youth pulsate in its literature, as though something unheard of, something which had never before been, must come into being."[30] When Francis Bacon wrote, "But that little vessels, like the celestial bodies, should sail round the whole globe, is the happiness of our age,"[31] he was apparently speaking of the wonderful geographical discoveries that were being made during the Renaissance, not university lectures on poetry or literature; yet the two may not have been unrelated. After all, the essence of the Renaissance was a spirit of adventure, a personal striving for excellence and meaningful achievement. In that sense, art and culture were being reborn. Humanist scholars had their own voyages of discovery to pursue. They hoped to use the revived classical learning as a launching platform from which men might sally forth on trailblazing voyages of the mind. "What a piece of work is man!" remarked one of the greatest intellects of the period. "In action how like an angel! In apprehension how like a god!" This vision of the liberated human spirit, to be sure, was not always realized in Renaissance classrooms or in humanist scholarly works. It nevertheless remained a noble one.

3

The Reformation

The professor, accompanied only by a faithful servant, approaches the church. Quickly he nails a long list of theses to the door, challenging all who wish to do so to debate with him the propriety and legality of papal indulgences. All of this is in strict conformity with university custom. The date is October 31, 1517; the place, Wittenberg; the professor, Martin Luther. Thus, in a quiet university town in Germany begins one of the most significant revolutions in the history of European civilization, the Protestant Reformation.

Thus from its inception, the Reformation was an affair of universities as well as of princes and prelates. This, of course, was inevitable. Church and university had been closely linked for centuries; no such thing as a purely secular university existed anywhere. There could not, then, be a revolution in the church without a corresponding upheaval in the universities.

At first Luther's challenge was ignored: no one came to debate him. Ultimately, though, his actions had momentous consequences. For a time he considered: should he publish the theses? He discussed the matter with a few close friends. In the meantime events moved swiftly out of his control. Somehow, other "university friends" got hold of the dynamite-laden propositions and promptly published them both in Latin and German. This was apparently done without Luther's personal authorization.[1] In any event, thousands of copies of the criticism of indulgences were soon circulating throughout the land, and not long after, printed copies of Luther's theses were attracting attention in the Netherlands, Switzerland, even England.[2]

As the indulgence controversy grew hotter, universities found it difficult to avoid involvement. The Dominican indulgence-seller, Johann Tetzel, whose high-pressure sales methods had triggered the whole affair, published a defense of his conduct. His 106 anti-theses were published by the press of the University of Frankfort. When the students at the University of Wittenberg obtained copies of this rebuttal, they heaped them up in a big pile and burned them.[3]

By this time the controversy was as much a battle of rival universities as of rival theology professors. Most of the professors at Wittenberg defended their colleague Martin Luther vigorously. On the other hand, Wittenberg's competitor in Saxony, the University of Leipsig, became a center of anti-Lutheranism. Dr. John Eck, a member of the faculty of the University of Ingolstadt, challenged the Lutherans to a public disputation. Eck, reputedly one of the most able debaters in Christendom, boasted that he would demolish Luther. The Wittenbergers quickly accepted Eck's challenge, and the University of Leipsig agreed to host the debate.[4]

The highly publicized confrontation took on the appearance of a tournament, but in this case university scholars rather than knights on horseback were the main participants. With much ceremony the duke of Saxony appeared to open the proceedings. Learned professors from the universities of Paris and Erfurt sat on the platform as official judges. Meanwhile careful security was provided for the participants. The Wittenbergers—Luther, Carlstadt, Melanchton, and others—arrived in Leipsig with an escort of two hundred or so brawny students armed with battle-axes. The red-faced, loud-voiced Eck, in turn, was protected night and day by a well-armed bodyguard of seventy-six constables provided by the town council.[5]

Somehow bloodshed was avoided and the Leipsig debate went on as scheduled. The resultant clash of theology professors proved to be one of the most significant university debates in history. Eck's sharp questions produced a hardening of Luther's position, and the Wittenberg professor found himself propelled toward a total and irrevocable break with the Roman Papacy. Thus, a national religious revolution was launched through channels made available by the university system of the day. The Lutheran Reformation had begun.

University teachers and graduates had been involved prominently in challenges to the church long before Luther's time. In fourteenth-century England, Oxford professor John Wycliffe attracted a large following when he translated the Bible into the vernacular and called for more direct access of the individual to God. These Wycliffian ideas soon spread to Bohemia (present-day Czechoslovakia). There Jan Hus, dean of the theological faculty and later rector of the University of Prague, led a national movement for religious reform. He was eventually declared by the Papacy to be a heretic and was executed at the Council of Constance.[6]

In the sixteenth century, university men all across

Europe played a leading role in the movement for religious reform. Ulrich Zwingli, the first important Reformation leader in Switzerland, was one of these. He had studied at the universities of Vienna and Basel, and had received a master's degree from the latter institution in 1502. Erasmus of Rotterdam was his idol and inspired the Swiss theologian to master Greek and other humanist studies. A contemporary of Zwingli also working for a religious revolution in Switzerland was William Farel. Farel was active in the French-speaking portions of the country. He had studied under Lefèvre d'Étaples at the University of Paris and later enrolled at the University of Basel.[7]

The most influential reformer in both France and Switzerland was John Calvin. Calvin like the Reformers already mentioned, was a university-trained scholar. For many years he studied scholastic philosophy and theology at the Sorbonne in Paris. There some of his classmates took note of his "censorious and fault-finding disposition" and nicknamed him "the accusative case." His father wished him to become a lawyer, and for a time Calvin studied law at the universities of Orleans and Bourges. All the while, like Zwingli, he was an avid student of humanist writings. Calvin's university background helps explain his important intellectual contributions to the theological literature of the Reformation. His learned treatise, *Institutes of the Christian Religion*, was considered by many to be the most scholarly and precise work produced by the sixteenth-century reformers.[8]

In England, too, more than a century after Wycliffe, university people played a notable role in the Reformation. A group of young Cambridge scholars, interested in the new Lutheran ideas that were filtering in from Germany, began to meet regularly for discussions at the White Horse Inn. The circle included Hugh Latimer, Fellow of Clare College; William Tyndale, a humanist newly arrived from Oxford; and Miles Coverdale, a student member of the Austin Friars. Others in this radical band, which for obvious reasons soon came to be dubbed "Little Germany," included Robert Barnes, Thomas Bilney, and future luminaries of the Church of England such as Thomas Cranmer. Ironically, Cardinal Wolsey, who was dedicated to stamping out all Lutheran sedition, unwittingly helped to spread it when he sponsored the migration of a group of able Cambridge men to a great new college he was planning at Oxford. Many of the students thus transplanted were members of the White Horse Inn set.[9]

During a time of upheaval, universities are usually shaken by pressures from the outside. This was eminently the case during the religious wars of the sixteenth century. Since the Reformation had many "revolutionary" aspects, it was bound to affect universities more drastically than the Renaissance had done. The Reformation, first of all, had an important effect on university enrollment. For a number of reasons, the enrollment trend at first turned sharply downward. The authorities in many areas confiscated ecclesiastical endowments that had been used for financial support of clerics at universities. Furthermore, bitter theological wrangling at some institutions drove away potential students. Then, too, with the priesthood discredited, parents no longer saw the pressing need to finance an expensive theological education for their sons. Statistics tell the sad story. At Rostock, for example, enrollment dropped from 300 in 1517 to 15 in 1525; at Erfurt, it declined from 311 in 1520 to 14 by 1525. At Basel only five students enrolled in 1526. The same depressing figures could be cited for Königsberg, Greifswald, Cologne, Mayence, Vienna, and many other institutions. In England, a steep decline set in at Oxford and Cambridge.[10]

These setbacks proved to be only temporary. Ultimately, greater numbers of students crowded into universities than before; equally important, many new universities were founded. What brought about this reversal of fortune? Reformation society obviously came to realize that higher education could not be lightly discarded, that indeed it was more essential than ever. Clergymen for the new reformed faiths had to be trained somewhere; governments needed increasing numbers of trained officials, and the rising middle class found higher education an indispensable means of preparing sons for careers in politics and business. In short, as the student clientele increased quantitatively, it also became more diverse in character.[11]

New universities sprang up all across sixteenth century Europe. Nine new institutions were founded in Germany, for example. Among these, Jena and Königsberg were established by Lutherans, Würzburg and Graz by Catholics. In Spain, two new institutions were established and the number of registered university students grew impressively. In Switzerland, Zwingli organized the University of Zurich and other Protestant leaders established the Academy or University of Geneva, with eminent theologian Theodor Beza as rector. The Geneva institution was successful from the start, attracting several hundred students the first year. Under Calvin's theocracy, the University of Geneva became the model for many other institutions of learning, including Leyden in the Netherlands, Edinburgh in Scotland, Emmanuel College, Cambridge, in England, and Harvard College in New England.

In the Netherlands the Dutch founded Franeker as well as Leyden during the later sixteenth century, even though their nation was involved at the time in a desperate struggle for independence. On the Counter-Reformation side, there were also efforts to establish new schools. The recently established Jesuit Order was active all over Europe, revitalizing old universities and creating new ones. In Germany, for example, the universities of Paderborn, Münster and Osnabrück, which came into existence at this time, were Jesuit foundations primarily.[12]

In the British Isles, the decline in enrollment was substantially reversed by the later decades of the sixteenth century, and two new institutions made their appearance—the University of Edinburgh (1583) and Trinity College, Dublin (1591). Furthermore, a number of new colleges were established at the two older universities: Corpus Christi, Brasenose, and Christ Church at Oxford; and Magdalen, Trinity, Sidney Sussex, and St. John's at Cambridge. The Crown professed to have only the kindest feelings toward the universities. King Henry VIII was quoted as saying: "I tell you, sirs, that I judge no land in England better bestowed than that which is given to our Universities. For by their maintenance our realme shall be well governed when we be dead and rotten."[13]

The Reformation, writes Arnold Toynbee, "substituted the intellectual authority of the local secular governments (cuius regio, eius religio) for the authority of the Catholic Church."[14] This trend meant that institutions of higher education more than ever would become instruments of the state. The claims of the state—whether national monarchy, petty principality, or municipality— necessarily overrode any claims the university might advance based on chartered rights or corporate autonomy. The university was obviously too vital to the state's purposes to be left at liberty; it performed a crucial role in training secular officials for the government's bureaucracy and clerical personnel for the established church. Therefore, all university activists were made subject to political supervision and all members of the university community were expected to conform to the official "party line." The parallel with the status of universities in the police states of the twentieth century is striking. As Protestant forces advanced or Catholic forces struck back, one side might seize control of the state apparatus only to have the other side shortly regain power. Meanwhile, the effects upon universities were often catastrophic. Professors were hired, fired, rehired. Whole faculties were dispersed. Professors, as state employees, were required to take an oath of loyalty not only to the prince or commonwealth but also to "the right, true, evangelical doctrine" (meaning whatever variety of Protestantism or Catholicism the government officially endorsed).

The religious wars of the times sometimes disrupted or dispersed student bodies as well. Even when this did not occur, students found themselves under more rigid restrictions than before. Very often, students from one locality were expressly forbidden to attend universities on the other side of the "denominational curtain." Philip II in 1559 forbade Spaniards to study abroad, except at the Universities of Bologna, Naples, Rome, and Coimbra. In 1570, the inhabitants of Franche-Comte were ordered by the French government to refrain from "studying, teaching, learning or residing in any universities or public or private schools other than in this country or other countries, states and realms in our obedience, excepting always the town and university of Rome." J. H. Elliott notes, in this connection, that "eighty or so universities of mid-sixteenth century Europe were being transformed from international into national institutions, and . . . the European community of scholars was itself being fragmented by the new confessional strife."[15]

However, many of the seemingly new departures in university policy that made their appearance in the sixteenth century may have been simply an elaboration of trends already well established. For example, the drive to found a number of new universities had precedents in the past. During pre-Reformation times, principalities and municipalities frequently vied with each other to obtain charters for universities, hoping that these new establishments would bring prestige and business to the parent communities. In similar fashion, the autonomy of universities had been encroached upon long before the Reformation. Writing about England, Joan Simon observes: "The universities had never been autonomous to the extent that has sometimes been suggested. Privileges always implied obligations and in the previous century Oxford had found that papal immunities could be of little account in times of stress as against the immediate demands of kings."[16]

We are discussing here differences of degree rather than kind, however, and beyond question the Reformation produced a significant tightening-up of political control over universities. England gives us a good example of this trend. Having broken with the Papacy, Henry VIII in 1535 made his chief minister, Thomas Cromwell, head of a royal commission to look into the affairs of Oxford and Cambridge. These institutions were not permitted to give aid or comfort to partisans of the Pope, who were now, in the King's eyes, traitors. The royal commission forced the universities to surrender their ancient charters, including all "papistical muniments," plus inventories of all university lands and other properties. Henceforth both faculty and curriculum would remain under the direct oversight of the privy council. Shortly thereafter, all monastic properties and monastic residences for students at Oxford and Cambridge were confiscated by order of the Crown. Finally, in 1553, all candidates for university degrees were required to subscribe to the Articles of Religion of the Church of England.

The royal commission proclaimed that there was a genuine need for reform at the universities. There were

ments outright. When this extreme measure was proposed to Henry VIII, he replied indignantly: "Ah sirra! I perceive the Abbey lands have fleshed you, and set your teeth on edge, to ask also those colleges."[21] Bluff Harry declared that, as far as the colleges were concerned, "he had not in his realme so many persons so honestly maytayned in lyvyng bi so little land and rent."[22]

By and large, the occasional meddling with universities by agents of the state in England was mild compared to the traumatic inquisitions that were then assailing the institutions of continental Europe. The duke of Saxony, for example, fired all the professors at the University of Leipsig who would not accept Lutheranism. The same mass housecleaning occurred at the University of Tubingen. Moreover, as the Reformation proceeded, feuds erupted within the Protestant camp itself, leading to still more academic quarrels. Lutherans conflicted sharply with followers of Zwingli and Calvin, and even within the Lutheran fold, serious differences of opinion developed. Disciples of Melanchthon, who were entrenched at Wittenberg, fought many battles against the followers of a rival theologian, Flacius Illyricus, whose faction was dominant at Jena. This controversy caused angry conflicts at several other German universities.[23]

An example of the intensity of feeling produced by these theological feuds comes from the University of Wittenberg in 1568. At that time, a student named Schlusselberg (later to win a measure of fame himself as a theologian) applied for the master's degree. One of the examining professors asked whether it was true that Schlusselberg had been telling gatherings of students that the professors at Wittenberg were just a bunch of perverted Calvinists. Schlusselberg denied these charges but admitted that, personally, he was not entirely satisfied with the orthodoxy of the faculty. Thereupon a university

allegedly large numbers of older clergymen in re
who were not engaged in serious study, "ne, ne
tending," but were spending their time gossiping in
of refreshment such as the Dolphin, the Bull, or the
Horse in Cambridge, "remaining in idleness and in
pastimes and indolent pleasures," all the while occup
the rooms and enjoying the "commodities" that had l
intended for "the relief and maintenance of p
scholars." A government mandate in 1536 separated su
"idlers" from their sinecures forthwith.[17]

During the 1570s, Queen Elizabeth's governme
promulgated tough new statutes for the universities, seek
ing to regulate the most minute aspects of college life
including times of lectures, degrees, disputations, even
the dress of students.[18] As the political pendulum swung
wildly back and forth during these years—from Henry
VIII's royal church and Edward VI's extreme Protestantism to the Catholic counterrevolution under Mary,
and finally the middle-of-the-road Anglicanism of
Elizabeth—university policy, of necessity, swung with it.
The constant theological wrangling and political uncer-
tainties accompanying it were hardly conducive to quiet
scholarship. Young Francis Bacon, thoroughly disgusted
with the situation, wrote that "the Controversies of the
Church" were "such as violate truth, sobriety or peace"
and charged that "the universities are the seat and continent of this disease, whence it hath been and is derived
into the rest of the realm."[19] Another contemporary, Matthew Parker, was similarly unhappy with the course of
events. "Scholars' controversies be now many and trou-
blous," he observed, "and their delight is to come before
men of authority to show their wits, etc."[20]

While nonconforming professors like Thomas
Cartwright, the arch-Puritan, were summarily dismissed,
the Crown chose not to confiscate the university endow-

council was convened and he was brought before it and ordered to make his views clear. Schlusselberg recorded his own recollection of these proceedings:

> Hereupon Dominus Casparus Peucerus asked me and said, "Hark ye, you follower of Flacius, I learn that you look upon me as a Calvinist and profaner of the sacrament; tell me this much to my face, and prove that I am a teacher of false doctrine." Thereupon I replied that I *did* hold him to be an unbelieving Calvinist and profaner of the Sacrament, and was ready to make good my belief out of his own *Praelections*. Thereupon he became angry beyond all measure, called me a Flacian knave, and begged the Rector to give him permission to stand up in order that he might box my ears. I however said that I was no Flacian knave, but an honorable man, and did not care whether a Calvinist praised me or reviled me. . . . Thereupon he exclaimed, "What, my fine fellow, is any one going to dispute with a Flacian knave like you!" And then turning to his colleagues, he said, "My dear colleagues, is not this sad and astonishing? How shall we excuse ourselves with men of discernment, if we allow it to go forth that a young coxcomb like this is allowed to reproach us to our faces?"

Schlusselberg was thereupon banished from the University of Wittenberg forever.[24]

Governments sought to avoid such wrangling by tightening their hold on the universities. The duke of Prussia, for example, demanded that all professors at the University of Königsberg swear an oath of fealty to him personally as well as to the state church. At Basel and Geneva the universities were put completely under the control of town magistrates and councils. At Vienna the university was subservient to the Hapsburg archdukes, with every detail of instruction subject to rigorous government inspection and review. The duke of Bavaria similarly imposed stringent controls on the University of Ingol-stadt. So it went throughout Reformation Germany and Switzerland, and practically everywhere else in Europe. Köningsberg and Geneva happened to be Protestant in-stitutions; Vienna and Ingolstadt were Catholic. The pat-tern, however, of university subjugation to the will of the state was substantially the same.[25]

The Reformation created other vexing problems as well. For some universities, finances became a source of grave anxiety. Church lands had been confiscated in most Protestant countries, and some of this wealth was sup-posed to have been reallocated for the support of universi-ties and other schools. This, however, did not always hap-pen. In earlier times, a number of teaching posts had been supported by church "livings"; these now frequently dis-appeared. The monastic residences at Oxford and Cam-bridge were suppressed. University endowments in Ger-many were from time to time confiscated by princes or town councils. Pay for professors was often reduced and at times disbursed rather irregularly. Molshem, a distin-guished professor of Greek at Heidelberg, petitioned the university in 1537, pleading that it was impossible to keep up appearances and support his family on the small salary he received. His pay was thereupon raised by one-third, but the prince, on hearing of this, suggested that he in-stead should have been fired. The sixteenth century was an era of runaway inflation, and some professors were forced to supplement their meagre incomes by moonlight-ing at other jobs. At Heidelberg, for example, the statutes of 1558 permitted professors to raise additional cash by retailing a stipulated quantity of wine each year.[26]

Students, too, frequently found themselves in more difficult straits than before. In Protestant countries, poor students who had lived in monastic houses or who had subsisted on church scholarships, were cast adrift. Some observers feared that under these circumstances serious students would become more scarce at the universities. In England more and more sons of the wealthy and influential were flocking there. "Knights, lords, and lawyers" replaced the "ragged clerks, weavers and butchers' sons" who had predominated at the colleges in earlier days.[27] Student residences became more luxurious; new, impressive quadrangles were built, and the simple attire of pre-Reformation days was replaced by fashionable hats and ruffs. Wealthy "fellow commoners"—sons of noblemen and country gentlemen—dined separately at High Table with the Fellows and lived in commodious lodgings. The ordinary "commoners"—sons of small businessmen or lesser squires—lived in much simpler style. At the bottom of the pyramid were the "battelers," who worked their way through by dispensing the daily beer, waiting on tables, working in the kitchen, or running errands.[28]

Constant theological disputes and political-ecclesiastical warfare made the lives of many professors precarious. In Italy, professors had enjoyed a certain amount of freedom during the Renaissance years, but the Counter-Reformation brought the Inquisition to the peninsula. All professors now had to take oaths swearing allegiance to Roman Catholicism, and at Naples they were even asked to affirm their support of the doctrine of the immaculate conception, a concept that had not yet become an official church dogma. At some Italian institutions humanistic studies now languished as more emphasis was placed on biblical instruction and Catholic theology. Despite such restrictions, some institutions retained a greater measure of freedom than others. Padua, for example, perhaps because it was protected by the Republic of Venice from Spanish or papal domination, remained an important center of scientific studies (Copernicus and Vesalius studied there).[29]

The vicissitudes in the life of an Italian professor during the Reformation years are illustrated dramatically in the case of Jerome Cardan. This eminent mathematician and physician, author of some 242 articles and books, was dismissed from his chair at the University of Milan and tried as a heretic. Imprisonment followed, and he was forced to witness the execution by torture of his favorite son, who was charged with gross immorality. Cardan proved to be remarkably durable, however. Somehow he survived, received an appointment as professor of medicine at the University of Bologna, and eventually qualified to receive a pension from the pope.[30]

In Spain, the Inquisition raged on unchecked. Guided by the Index of forbidden literature, all textbooks were reviewed for signs of heresy and rigorously censored. Teachers were spied on and apprehended if they deviated in any way from the orthodox Catholic line. The power of the Inquisitors was demonstrated graphically in the case of Ponce de León, a noted poet-scholar and professor of theology at the University of Salamanca. Ponce de León was charged with heresy because of a new and allegedly worldly translation that he had made of the Song of Songs. Thrown into prison for five years and tortured, he somehow managed to survive and, after an admonition, gained his release. He thereupon promptly returned to his teaching at the university, resuming his lectures at the precise point where they had been interrupted when he was arrested, remarking cooly to his class, "As I was saying at the last time."[31]

In divided Germany conditions were not much better.[32] At Protestant Wittenberg after 1592, all professors were required to subscribe to the Lutheran Augsburg Con-

fession unreservedly; at Catholic Vienna, all members of
the theological faculty were required to base their teaching
exclusively on Peter Lombard's *Sentences* and the writings
of other Catholic dogmatists. The noted mathematician
and astronomer, Johann Kepler, was forced as a Protestant to leave his position at the University of Graz, but
later managed to rejoin his scientific associate, Tycho
Brahe, in Prague. Botanist Leonhard Rauwolf of Augsburg
returned to his home in 1576 only to be driven out because
of his Protestantism. At the University of Cracow in Po-
land, Alexander Zuchta, a pupil of Paracelsus, was found
guilty of heresy, stripped of his academic hood, and ex-
iled.[33]

In France, wars of religion raged through the land
during the latter half of the sixteenth century, and the
universities were expected to hew the orthodox line in all
matters. When a few University of Paris professors later
came under the influence of Cartesian philosophy, the
government dispatched the archbishop to tell them that
they must abandon such novel doctrines. The Parlement
of Paris, for its part, prohibited a scheduled university
debate on anti-Aristotelian theses, thus disappointing an
audience of a thousand. The Sorbonne during these years
condemned and refused publication licenses to nearly all
the important scientific and scholarly works of the period.
Meanwhile, every new college and university that the Huguenot Calvinists set up was forcibly suppressed. Huguenot scientists such as Le Paulmier and Grevin were
deprived of their doctorates and forced to flee the country.
Finally, in 1600 the government made its control of
academic life total and permanent. King Henry IV an-
nounced at that time that henceforth the University of
Paris was to be supervised directly by the state. Every
aspect of its curriculum and academic procedure would be
regulated in minute detail.[34]

England, as we have seen, also placed university professors under close scrutiny, but perhaps somewhat less rigorously than was the case on the Continent. It is true that in 1575 it was proclaimed that no Roman Catholic might remain at Oxford or Cambridge. There was a difference, however, between what appeared on the statute books and what was actually enforced. University men who were only halfhearted in their conformity or who eventually showed themselves to be "Romanists" were permitted for many years to retain their posts. Caius College, Cambridge, for a time acquired the reputation of being "a nursery of papists." Mark H. Curtis maintains that "outward conformity and seeming order rather than unconditional assent to a theological position were the objects" for which the authorities pressed.[35] Be that as it may, the ultimate effect of the English regulations was to make Oxford and Cambridge thoroughly Anglican.

How, in the face of these sectarian and political difficulties, did the higher learning manage to survive? As a matter of fact, things turned out better than might have been expected. To a certain extent, continuity with university traditions was maintained. Theological studies were now emphasized much more than before, but at the same time, the humanistic curriculum was preserved in many institutions. The traditional organization of faculties dating back to the medieval period remained the same. The classical curriculum continued to be important for the training of clergymen, public officials, even would-be gentlemen. It is also noteworthy that serious university work in the ancient Oriental languages began during this period. Because of the new concern for Hebrew and other Near Eastern tongues, important scholarly work began to appear in the field of biblical studies. An outstanding example was the King James Bible, compiled in the early seventeenth century by a group of learned English Hebraists and Hellenists who had been recruited mainly from the universities.[36]

Nor did the bitter controversies of the era completely inhibit explorations of other fields of knowledge. During the 1540s the University of Wittenberg acquired the reputation of being a center of liberal learning, attracting brilliant students from abroad such as Tycho Brahe, William Tyndale, and Giordano Bruno, but later in the century the controversies between Philippists and Flacians disrupted the institution's academic atmosphere. Before this happened, however, Rheticus, a professor of mathematics at Wittenberg and a former student of Copernicus, had published the first account in print (1540) of his mentor's heliocentric theory. Reinhold, a professor of astronomy and colleague of Rheticus, compiled the first astronomical tables based on the Copernican theory about this time. These were published in 1551 under the title *The Prussian Tables*.[37] In England, too, scientific studies went on at the universities during the Reformation years. Thomas Harriott and Nathaniel Torporley worked in mathematics and astronomy, William Barlow made studies of magnets, Sir Henry Saville delivered lectures on astronomy, and Richard Hakluyt lectured on geography and navigation.[38]

Inevitably, different emphases developed within Protestant and Catholic universities. Protestant institutions appear to have been somewhat more hospitable to studies in the natural sciences than were the Catholic ones.[39] Notwithstanding this difference, useful work was done by both Catholic and Protestant scientists during the Reformation period.[40] In the field of law, an important difference was that Protestant universities dropped completely the study of canon law, replacing it with civil law. In philosophy, too, changes were proposed. Some Protestant scholars wished to replace the medieval Aristotelian system with a new logical method introduced by Petrus Ramus. In this case, however, tradition proved to be too deeply rooted to be changed significantly. Philip Melanchthon and other Lutheran scholars developed a modified humanistic form of Aristotelian scholasticism and this eventually became the philosophic norm at many Protestant universities.[41]

H. Richard Niebuhr speaks of the Reformation era as ushering in a new burst of freedom, shattering the medieval power structure beyond repair, and paving the way for the more pluralistic "modern nationalist, democratic and capitalistic cultures."[42] It is questionable whether this statement applies to the universities of the sixteenth and early seventeenth centuries, however. In its *immediate* impact, the Reformation proved to be disastrous for many of the universities. As we have observed, faculties were divided and disrupted. Student ability to move freely from university to university was seriously inhibited. The Inquisition and the Index cowed many university scholars into silence. To be sure, some found ingenious ways of getting around the system. But an age in which Bruno was burned and Galileo was forced to recant presented great difficulties for original thought and advancement of knowledge. As in our own troubled century, the universities of the Reformation were harassed by bitter ideological and political conflicts. The Reformation was a time of upheaval, and inevitably universities were made to pay a price. But, in spite of it all, they survived, and perhaps their survival is the single most important fact that emerges from this era of university history.

4

Absolutism and Enlightenment

We live in a world that has been shaped in countless ways by science and the national state. When Paul von Fuchs, at the opening of the University of Halle in 1694, asked, "Where do you find a nation which has become mighty without science?" he had recognized that the interaction of science and national development already exercised a decisive influence on civilization. By his time, national bureaucracies were expanding rapidly, and the combination of natural science and the cultural "enlightenment" was having a revolutionary impact upon the world of thought. Just as in earlier periods of significant change, universities were affected significantly by the new currents. Only a relatively small minority of them, however, reacted meaningfully to the intellectual developments of the age. Leyden and Utrecht, Halle and Göttingen, Edinburgh and Glasgow, and to some extent, Vienna, were in this category. Other eighteenth-century universities were far less responsive to science and enlightenment; they still retained narrow and antiquated curriculums and methodologies, made few contributions to thought, and opposed the ideologies spawned by the Enlightenment.

By and large, it was the *newer* universities—schools such as Halle and Göttingen—that proved most receptive to new ideas. Older, well-established institutions (for example, Paris and Louvain) tended to hang back. In addition, universities in Holland and other highly urbanized countries were more likely to accommodate themselves to new social and intellectual realities than were more isolated institutions.[1]

Advocates of the new learning grew impatient with the disinclination of many universities to change their ways. Methods of instruction had scarcely been modified since medieval times; rarely were recent works assigned as texts or experiments employed as part of the regular course work. Scientists and scholars of a more adventurous temper had to look outside of university halls for intellectual stimulation. Few important scientific discoveries were made by university professors. Few of the revolutionary industrial techniques that were beginning to transform the European economy were being developed at universities. Critics were tempted to heap their scorn on institutions they could only regard as antiquated and obtuse the way an English booster of technologically oriented education did in 1667:

> Oxford and Cambridge are our laughter
> Their learning is but pedantry;
> These collegiates do assure us,
> Aristotle's an ass to Epicurus.[2]

What was to be done? With university doors closed to new thought, where could a congenial environment be found for intellectual exploration? For a time, scholars had recourse to a whole new set of learned institutions: the scientific societies. Following Italian Renaissance models, a number of these institutions were established in the seventeenth century, including the Royal Society of London, the Académie des Sciences of Paris, and the Accademia del Cimento of Florence. After 1700, many other scientific societies were founded, often with the enthusiastic support of monarchs and governments. Some appeared in remote provincial cities, others in faraway colonies (American Philosophical Society, Philadelphia, 1743). Some of them preferred to specialize, serving the needs of just one branch of science.

In essence, the learned academies and scientific societies functioned as parallel institutions to the universities. They disseminated knowledge by publishing scholarly journals and issued bulletins of research in progress. They organized lectures and experimental demonstrations, and awarded prizes to promising scholars.[3]

The English Universities

A number of prominent universities resisted the new trends of the seventeenth and eighteenth centuries, however. Oxford and Cambridge, for example, were practically somnolent, reaching their all-time low point during the middle years of the eighteenth century. David Ogg describes them as "little more than annexes to the established church."[4] Their teachers, in the main, did all they could to ignore modern studies.[5] Their wealthier students, who made these schools a favorite gathering place, took life easy as they socialized with one another, sparing themselves the difficulties of study or thought. Edward Gibbon, the celebrated historian, experienced these conditions personally during his residence at Oxford. He could only conclude that the English universities, having been founded in the Middle Ages, "a dark age of false and barbarous science," showed very little evidence as yet that they were able to overcome the handicaps of their origin.[6]

It is all the more ironic that during these years a few truly great scholars remained on the staffs of the English universities. But these brilliant intellects (Isaac Newton was one) had only a minimal influence on the actual teaching that was going on at these institutions. Maurice Ashley suggests that the critical weakness of the seventeenth- and eighteenth-century English university may not have been in its scholarship *per se*, but in its performance as an educational institution.[7] The only contact, for example, between Oxford or Cambridge and the Royal Society was through scientists, such as Newton, Cotes, Halley, and Bradley, who happened to be teaching at the universities and were active in the society on their own account. There was no permanent institutional arrangement. The notable researches of Oxford or Cambridge professors got no support from university administrators and had little impact on teaching. A typical example was the situation of eighteenth-century Cambridge physicist and chemist Henry Cavendish. Cavendish carried on his principal research in London, not at his university, and his scientific investigations had little impact on his classes.

There were a few developments, however, that foreshadowed the more diverse university involvements of later times. In 1683, Ashmolean Hall was completed at Oxford and subsequently was made available for the teaching of science. Important, too, was the publication at Oxford in 1702 of the first university textbook based on the principles of Newtonian mathematics and physics: David Gregory's *Astronomiae, Physicae et Geometriae Elementa*. Then, in 1747, another modern discipline was given university recognition when a chair in modern history was established at Oxford. At Cambridge, meanwhile, between 1702 and 1783 regular chairs were established in chemistry, botany, geology, and "experimental philosophy."

At this time, though, a more innovative education was provided, not by the universities, but by the so-called dissenting, or Nonconformist, academies. After the Restoration of the Stuarts in 1661, Oxford and Cambridge were closed to all Nonconformists (dissenters from the Church of England). Consequently, non-Anglicans were forced to create their own educational institutions where their sons could pursue work of university grade. A number of academies were founded specifically to perform that function, although such institutions still lacked the authority to grant university degrees. Some of them, such as Warrington, Daventry, and Hackney, nonetheless became widely renowned for the high quality of their work.

The Nonconformist academies often combined secondary-school and college-level work under the same roof. Since they were not concerned with the preparation of students for entrance to the classicist-dominated university, they could afford a more experimental curriculum than was customary at traditional schools. They could, and did, teach many modern subjects neglected elsewhere: geography, modern history, modern languages, and, of course, the natural sciences.[8]

The educational philosophy of Bohemian reformer John Amos Comenius was quite influential in shaping the pedagogical outlook of the Nonconformist academies. Comenius emphasized the importance of studying *realia*— real things in the world of science and technology. The English Puritans and Nonconformists were greatly impressed by Comenius's empiricist approach and sought to apply it in their institutions. Northampton Academy, for example, taught such subjects as mechanics and hydrostatics with the aid of experimental demonstrations and student observations.[9] Thriving academies such as Daventry and Warrington, "the Athens of the North," were located in industrial towns and tried to make their courses serve the economic needs of their communities. "Here, then," notes one historian, "was the union between science and industry [that was] so prophetic for the future."[10] Prominent industrialists in Manchester, Liverpool, and Birmingham donated the money that brought Warrington Academy into being in 1757.

Eventually the word got about that graduates of the dissenting academies, because of their broader curriculum, had a better chance than Oxford or Cambridge graduates of securing jobs in the expanding British civil service—especially positions in the customs and excise divisions. At that point, even Anglican parents began to send their sons to these schools. Not all of the academies were high-quality educational institutions, however. Some were ephemeral, private-venture enterprises offering rather superficial training. But those which did respectable work had distinguished men on their teaching staffs—men of the stature of Joseph Priestley, discoverer of oxygen, John Dalton, formulator of the atomic theory, and the pioneer statistician, Richard Price. Whatever their shortcomings, the Nonconformist academies helped develop scientific and technical training to serve the needs of England's Industrial Revolution, something the established universities were not yet ready to do.[11]

The French Universities

Turning now to the French universities, a paradox quickly appears: France was the vital center of the eighteenth-century Enlightenment, but her universities lagged far behind. French higher learning under the Old Regime was arid, obscurantist, and reactionary. Gershoy calls the twenty-two French universities of that day "bastions of learned ignorance."[12] They were tightly controlled by theologians (reactionary ones, at that) and closely supervised by the Bourbon government. The authorities disapproved of educational innovations and would not permit the discussion of controversial issues. They banned books considered to be "subversive," including such contemporary works as Montesquieu's *Spirit of the Laws*, Helvétius's *De L'Esprit*, and Rousseau's *Emile*. Theodore Zeldin notes that by this period of time standards in the nation's faculties of theology, law, and medicine "had fallen abysmally low, as had the number of students in them. Many professors had abandoned lecturing altogether, and confined themselves to the lucrative task of issuing degrees." Things became so bad that serious students sued their professors to force them to lecture. But this situation did not disturb the majority of French students; they simply did not bother to attend class.[13]

Such conditions could not be excused on the ground that French universities had more to do with contemporary scientific research than with teaching. Here, too, they did little. The Académie des Sciences in Paris, one of Europe's leading centers of scientific experimentation, had scarcely any connection with the University of Paris or any other French university.[14] A number of special schools were established after 1750 to compensate for these deficiencies—military academies, schools of mineralogy, and institutes concerned with engineering and road construction. Furthermore, unlike their German counterparts, the French universities had no special programs to train administrators for service to the state.[15]

The failure of the universities caused a lively alternative culture to spring up to meet the intellectual needs of the French Enlightenment. In eighteenth-century France this "counterculture" assumed many forms: world-famous Paris salons, specialized literary and scientific societies, controversial journals of opinion, and the widely acclaimed works produced by the Encyclopedists. Perhaps the best commentary on the intellectual level of the French universities is that few figures of the French Enlightenment ever attended them.

The Dutch Universities

The adjustment of universities to modern civilization went further in seventeenth-century Holland, a little nation in the forefront of the commercial and urban revolution, than in France. The Dutch universities won a deserved reputation as important centers of scientific study and scholarly research. Scholars such as Lipsius, Grotius, and Scaliger used them as their base of operations. In the following century these institutions retained their scientific renown, although the quality of their teaching may have deteriorated somewhat. W. J. s'Gravesande, appointed professor of mathematics and astronomy at Leyden in 1716, became the first university teacher on the Continent to base his instruction exclusively on Newton's discoveries. At this time, too, the Dutch institutions were doing important work in the medical sciences, developing such fields as chemistry, botany, zoology, and anatomy as reputable scientific disciplines.

In 1709 Herman Boerhaave was appointed professor of medicine at Leyden; soon thereafter the medical school of that university won the reputation of being Europe's best. Boerhaave's theories were, for a time, enormously influential. In addition, he trained a number of disciples who spread his concepts to the universities of Edinburgh, Vienna, and Göttingen. The Leyden system of medical training stressed a number of things: a close connection between teaching and research; a requirement that medical students master basic sciences before proceeding with specialized training; the institution of new university chairs in various scientific disciplines; the measurement of student achievement by means of rigorous examinations; and excellent facilities for research, including chemical laboratories, botanical gardens, and clinics in hospitals.[16]

The Dutch universities played such a key role in advancing the scientific revolution and the Enlightenment that one is almost tempted to overlook a few negative aspects. The influence of the Dutch Reformed Church remained strong at the universities and as a result dogmatic considerations sometimes interfered with scientific work. As a case in point, Gerhard van Swieten, a renowned physiologist trained at Leyden, was denied a professorial chair there because he was a Roman Catholic. Van Swieten eventually moved to Austria and became the chief educational advisor to the Hapsburgs and founder of the University of Vienna's school of medicine. Furthermore, the most creative Dutch scientists of this period were not usually members of university faculties. Christian Huygens, Jan Swammerdam, and Anthonij van Leeuwenhoeck, key figures in the seventeenth-century scientific revolution, never taught at the Dutch universities. Huygens was a gentleman-scientist of independent means and international reputation, and at that time a university chair was apparently too humble a position to attract a man of his background. On the other hand, neither Swammerdam, the son of an apothecary, nor Leeuwenhoeck, who lacked both university training and independent income, had the expertise in Latin that was considered indispensable for anyone presuming to teach in a Dutch university. J. L. Price notes: "Only in the universities was the supremacy of Latin still unchallenged, and this was especially true of the universities of the Dutch Republic."[17] By the eighteenth century, however, leading scientists such as Herman Boerhaave finally gained recognition in these institutions.

The Scottish Universities

In the period of the Enlightenment, perhaps the closest ties that the Dutch universities established with foreign institutions were those with the universities of Scotland. The four Scottish schools—St. Andrews, Glasgow, Aberdeen, and Edinburgh—provided a nonresidential, relatively inexpensive, higher education much like that of Holland. Even more important, in these schools new fields of knowledge were explored and, wherever possible, theory was linked to practice. The Dutch professor Boerhaave, "teacher of half the chemists of Europe," had a large number of Scottish students, and these disciples worked to introduce modern scientific courses into the curriculum of their own universities.[18]

By the middle of the eighteenth century many contemporaries felt that the Scottish universities were offering the best higher education in the British Isles. They resembled the English dissenting academies because they did not draw a sharp line between a practical education and the traditional classical variety. At Aberdeen, for example, it was considered appropriate to offer courses in French and bookkeeping. Conservative critics denounced this curricular flexibility, charging that the Scottish institutions were really secondary schools. The students kept coming in large numbers, however, and by 1750 few could deny that in fields such as medicine, the sciences, and mathematics (if not in the classics) the universities of Scotland had few rivals.

An important change in the Scottish system came in 1708 when the University of Edinburgh abolished its antiquated regent system, under which all the professors had taught the entire curriculum. With the way cleared for specialization, important new university chairs were established. Universal civil history was separated from ecclesiastical history in 1719, and rhetoric and belles lettres was introduced in 1760. A Faculty of Law was established in 1722, with separate chairs in public law, civil law, and Scots law.

Many talented scholars and scientists—for example, Adam Smith, Dugald Stewart, Francis Hutcheson, and William Cullen—were associated with the eighteenth-century Scottish universities. In this connection, J. T. Merz notes a significant trend: "Whilst in England modern science was cultivated outside the pale of the universities, . . . all eminent Scotch men of science . . . were university professors."[19] This was demonstrated graphically at the medical school of Edinburgh, which became the special glory of that institution. Efforts were made to secure the best available scientists for its faculty: two brilliant chemists, William Cullen and Joseph Black, were lured away from Glasgow. Under their guidance, Edinburgh's medical school gained world renown for its courses on clinical medicine, which were given in conjunction with the Royal Infirmary and the Surgeon's Hospital.[20]

There were many other first-rate minds at the eighteenth century Scottish universities. Francis Hutcheson, professor of moral philosophy at Glasgow, was a key figure in the movement that introduced into Scotland ideas derived from the European Enlightenment.[21] Adam Ferguson's lectures, first at Glasgow and later at Edinburgh, pioneered the new field of social relations that later came to be called sociology. His successor at Edinburgh, Dugald Stewart, helped to elaborate the widely influential

Scottish "Common Sense" school of philosophy, which later had a significant impact on American higher education.[22] These men of learning helped to create a "Scottish Enlightenment" that gained worldwide attention.[23] Nicholas Phillipson observes: "Edinburgh's literati and its university gave the city its well-known and remarkable international reputation as a center of learning from the 1760's onward and allowed Edinburgh to appear in foreign eyes as the Athens of the North." By this time, Edinburgh's university was playing a role comparable to that of Leyden a century earlier as a vital part of "a Republic of Letters, . . . The Athens of Britain."[24]

As the reputation of Scottish universities soared, students from other countries flocked to them. Edinburgh and the other Scottish schools eventually dropped all religious tests for admission, which further stimulated the influx. "Anglican and Presbyterian, Baptist and Quaker, Unitarian and Deist," notes David Horn, "were equally welcome to all faculties except Divinity."[25] As a result, a number of students from England and Northern Ireland began to attend the Scottish universities. These were soon joined by a sizable contingent from the West Indies and the British colonies of North America, most of whom enrolled in the University of Edinburgh's medical school.[26]

The New Social Sciences

Is the idea that a university must serve directly the needs of government and community (the "service-station" concept) peculiarly modern? Not necessarily. In seventeenth- and eighteenth-century central and northern Europe, universities were already performing such functions by training administrators and analyzing economic data. As national absolutism was perfected, governments required a larger and larger bureaucracy to realize their objectives. At this point, the university emerged as an indispensable instrument of the *Polizeistaat*.

The emergence of a corps of administrators trained in the universities took place in the sixteenth century. J. H. Elliott observes that by that time Europe had experienced "the first great age of government by paper. Everywhere the stacks of documents piled up, as more and more government business was consigned to carefully-written records kept by a growing army of clerks. Government by paper was the preserve of the professions—the clerk, the secretary, the trained civil servant. . . ."[27] To train these professionals, universities introduced programs in such new fields as public law, political economy, history, and applied science, and thus became "major avenues for the modernization of public life."[28]

Prussia is perhaps the best example of this line of development. The Hohenzollern princes of Brandenburg-Prussia were anxious to overcome the disastrous effects of the Thirty Years War (1618–1648) upon their domains and to expand their nation's influence in European affairs.[29] To achieve these ambitious goals they needed a more efficient public administration; this they proposed to secure through a renovated educational system and a liberal immigration policy. An important part of their strategy involved religious toleration because it would encourage the emigration to Prussia of Huguenot craftsmen and scholars whose skills could benefit the state. Accordingly, attacks by the orthodox Lutheran clergy on Pietists, Calvinists, or even philosophical rationalists attracted little support from the Hohenzollern government.[30]

A number of diverse intellectual trends—Pietism, science, and Natural-Law philosophy—thus were united in the late seventeenth century to produce an important new Prussian institution—the University of Halle. This project,

which had the full support of the king, was primarily
sponsored by two groups, the Pietists and the rationalists.

The Pietists, a Central European movement somewhat like the English Puritans and Nonconformists, were
religious reformers. They were opposed by the Lutheran
church establishment because of their crusade for a more
vital, less formalistic religion. Like their English counterparts, the Pietists were willing to follow new paths in education. One of their most influential leaders, August Her-
mann Francke, had supported the "moderns" in their
contemporary scholarly quarrel with the "ancients" and
was genuinely interested in a broad, empirically oriented
curriculum, much like that advocated by Comenius. Of
course, he also wished such a curriculum to be thoroughly
infused with the religious principles of Pietism. Francke
became Professor of Hebrew and Greek at Halle and was
one of the dominant personalities there from the earliest
days.[31]

The other mainstay of the new university was its professor of law, Christian Thomasius. He represented the
strain of mild rationalism and Natural Law philosophy
that was prominent at Halle from the beginning. At the
University of Leipsig Thomasius had taught law and philosophy and, beginning in 1688, had published a pe-
riodical that ridiculed the traditional university system.
Much university learning, he insisted, was useless ped-
antry, hiding behind outmoded teaching methods and an
antiquated language. Thomasius also broke with precedent by appearing in contemporary attire, discarding the
traditional academic gown. He pushed his nonconformity
too far, however, when he defended religious toleration
for Calvinists and other non-Lutherans. After a bitter
polemical exchange between Thomasius and the royal
chaplain of Denmark, the Danish government ordered

that his writings be burned by the public hangman and demanded that the Saxon government take measures to punish his insolence. Ultimately, Thomasius lost his professorship at Leipsig and forfeited his license to publish his journal. Threatened with further prosecution and even imprisonment, he fled the country and in 1690 sought asylum in Berlin. Frederick III welcomed the refugee scholar and permitted him to give a series of highly successful lectures on logic and law to young Prussian noblemen at the Ritterakademie of Halle. Eventually Frederick agreed to support Thomasius's ambitious plan (which also attracted strong Pietist backing) to elevate Halle's nobles' academy from secondary school to full university status.[32]

The new university received its formal charter in 1694. Thomasius declared at that time: "We are not bound to Aristotle; we shall not be accused of *lesé majesté* even if we make fun of the king of philosophers and philosopher of kings." From the start Halle sponsored a modern "utilitarian" program, which was probably the main reason that the Prussian state supported it enthusiastically. The study of ancient languages and literature was not emphasized as much as was customary at the time, and simultaneously modern languages, jurisprudence, and science were given increased attention.[33] The resultant "clever mixture of cosmopolitan spirit and modern legal training," began to attract law students from Germany's wealthier classes. The Halle formula turned out to be a highly popular combination of a "gentleman's education" (including instruction in riding, fencing, and music) with systematic preparation for a career in public administration.[34] Thomasius and Francke and the other members of the faculty lectured in the vernacular rather than in Latin. Science professors such as Ernst Stahl, the formulator of the influential "phlogiston" theory, stressed above all else the practical applications of scientific knowledge. Most important from the government's point of view, Halle emerged as the principal training school for the Prussian civil service.[35]

In 1727, King Frederick William I decreed that a new professorship be established at Halle in "Cameralia, Oeconomica, and Polizeisachen" (economics, administrative law, and public administration). The traditional juristic training, the king feared, was inadequate to train administrators who could build up the country's economy, so he asked Halle to pioneer the new field of *Kameralwissenschaft*(Cameralia) or public administration. Peter Simon Gasser was appointed the first professor of this budding science. Soon he published a textbook in which he defined *Okonomie* as pertaining to agriculture and associated industries, including "grain export, furnishing raw materials for domestic industry, . . . animal husbandry, . . . management of mills and forests." He understood Cameralia to mean "the counting house, including financial administration, budgeting, accounting, taxes, . . . (and) the acquisition of bullion in this mercantilistic age." *Polizeisachen* he stated was "the regulation of industry, commerce, urban life, public buildings, bridges, dikes, roads, and guilds."

The eighteenth-century Cameralists, themselves often successful businessmen, strove to increase the state's wealth and population in order to secure more efficient and honest tax collection, and to eradicate feudalistic privileges and exemptions that interfered with national economic growth. The Cameralists viewed public administration as a field for highly trained experts only, not for amateurs no matter how highly placed they might be. This explains their interest in university programs to train future administrators—programs that anticipated the present-day fields of public administration and business administration.[36]

Halle was a success from its very first year. Students

came to it in great numbers. Between the year of its founding, 1694, and 1728 no less than 18,208 students matriculated at Halle, more than at any other German university. As a result of the Pietists' influence, an orphanage, a dispensary, and a bible institute were set up near the university. In addition, an influential press was established in Halle—the Waisenhaus Press—whose textbooks, journals, and learned treatises circulated throughout northern Germany.

In 1747 another significant spin-off from the Halle experiment occurred. Johann Julius Hecker, a disciple of Francke's, established a pioneering school in Berlin, the Okonomisch-mathematische Realschule. This new kind of secondary school made "practical" studies its dominant concern. The school launched the whole utilitarian-oriented movement of Realschulen in German education.[37]

Another significant development at eighteenth-century Halle was the maintenance of a certain amount of academic freedom. The Halle professors, as learned men and specialists, were free to think for themselves and teach as they saw fit, as long as this was strictly within their field of professional and scholarly competence. This sounds fine, but in practice it turned out that freedom of teaching had distinct limits. Eventually, tensions built up between the rationalist wing on one hand and the Pietist faction on the other. The controversey centered on the teachings of Professor Christian Wolff, a world-famous philosopher who was even more of a rationalist than Thomasius. The Pietists complained to King Frederick William I that Wolff's determinist system would not only undermine religion and morality but would also destroy discipline in the army and the state. The Pietists won that battle when the alarmed ruler ordered Wolff to leave Prussian soil within forty-eight hours "on pain of immediate death." The rationalists had the final say, however, for by the time Frederick II ("the Great") became sovereign in the middle of the eighteenth century, the balance of power on the Halle faculty had shifted back to them. From 1740, Halle emerged as one of the leading centers of the German *Aufklarung* (Enlightenment), and Christian Wolff rejoined its faculty in triumph.

The contemporary English and French universities did not follow Halle's example with respect to public administration training, but a few schools in northern and central Europe did.[38] The University of Leipsig, for example, established a Cameralist chair soon after the one at Halle was created. The University of Uppsala in Sweden founded a similar professorship in 1740, and the Austrian Empire became very active in this field.

Under Empress Maria Theresa, Joseph von Sonnenfels emerged as the most influential teacher of Austria's future bureaucrats, introducing an extensive program of "cameral science" at the University of Vienna. Professors at the university's law faculty served as government advisors as well as teachers, functioning as a kind of eighteenth-century "brain trust." Maria Theresa was succeeded by Joseph II, and during his reign the utilitarian trend at the university continued. Joseph visualized higher education primarily as a training program for public administrators, and he reduced the number of universities in Austria to three, declaring that there were too many useless scholars and erudites in the country. Juridical, medical, and theological faculties expanded under his rule, while humanistic faculties shrank. Law professors were expected to emphasize public administration above all else. Only officially approved textbooks could be used and only government approved courses could be taught. Observing the rigid bureaucratic regimentation of students at the University of Vienna under this dispensation,

Mirabeau exclaimed, "Good God, even their souls are to be put in uniform!"[39]

Somewhat less extreme, but also following in the footsteps of Halle, was a new university in the Electorate of Hanover, the University of Göttingen. The Elector of Hanover in the middle of the eighteenth century also reigned in England as King George II. His German domains were ruled in his absence by an aristocratic council that inevitably came under English influence. Not surprisingly, some liberal ideas began to reach Hanover via England. In 1737, one of the Hanoverian ministers of state, Gerlach Adolph von Munchhausen, induced King George to establish a new institution of higher learning at the town of Göttingen. It is noteworthy that Munchhausen himself had studied at Halle and that his educational ideas bore an unmistakable Halle imprint. This is significant because not only was he the founder of the new university, but for the next thirty-three years he was the most important single influence on its development. Munchhausen labored during these years to build an institution where, above all, "the rulers and statesmen of the coming generation should be instructed in the political sciences and in the lessons of history, imbued with an enlightened spirit and trained in the practical application of what they had been taught."[40]

To realize Munchhausen's objectives, *Kameralwissenschaft* was given special attention from the very beginning. Students destined in later years to be prominent officials in their own countries came from distant lands to attend Göttingen's public administration lectures. These students helped contribute a distinct aristocratic flavor to Göttingen. Charles McClelland has shown that "not only were nobles represented at Göttingen disproportionately to the population, they were also there in much higher numbers than at other universities."[41] At the same time, Göttingen offered a rich variety of other courses—history, modern literature, science, medicine, chemistry, metallurgy, even agriculture. It was a broad curriculum and one that was in touch with the contemporary world. The needs of the resident aristocrats were also provided for by extensive training in the courtly arts of dancing, drawing, music, riding, and fencing. To aid its various teaching programs, the university provided an abundance of excellent physical facilities: well-equipped science laboratories, an astronomical observatory, an anatomical theater, a botanical garden, a museum of antiquities, and a university hospital. Most important, perhaps, was the university's splendid library, which grew within twenty years to house some sixty thousand books and one hundred thousand pamphlets—the best in Europe at that time. The library's manuscript index alone ultimately filled eighty-six volumes.[42]

Because of the superior library and laboratory resources, Göttingen's students did more independent reading and its professors did more original research than those at other eighteenth-century universities. Professor J. M. Gesner's philological seminar at Göttingen appears to have been the first advanced class of this type in the history of German higher learning. Professor J. S. Putter's lectures on *Reichsprozess*, or imperial trial law, made a significant contribution to the analysis and eventual codification of German law. Talented scholars were attracted to the university's staff by the offer of decent salaries, adequate pensions, and relative freedom to pursue their specialties. The result was that Göttingen's professors published extensively during these years. Their work in literary criticism and in classical archaeology was acclaimed throughout Europe, and the university's medical school was reputed to be one of the most distinguished of the era. Important contributions to scientific knowledge were made by such Göttingen teachers as the noted physiologist and botanist, Albrecht von Haller. A number of the university's science professors eventually banded together to found the famous Academy of Science in the town.[43]

The Emergence of a New Mission

The main question that remains, however, is: What part did European higher education *as a whole* play in the rise of modern science and, more specifically, in the emerging Age of Reason? All indications suggest that the achievements of Leyden, Edinburgh, Halle, and Göttingen were *not* duplicated widely elsewhere.[44] Even those progressive schools were primarily caught up in one side of the Enlightenment—the utilitarian and pragmatic side. Universities had little to do with the other, unsettling, but equally vital side—social reconstruction and revolutionary ideology and philosophy. In short, higher education during the Enlightenment stayed away from many areas where new and unconventional modes of thought were transforming the European mind.

In response to community desires and governmental mandates the more progressive universities of the time sponsored such noncontroversial and socially useful fields as public administration, applied science, medical science, economics, animal husbandry, scientific agriculture, and public finance. In so doing, they contributed significantly to the wealth and power of the "enlightened" monarchies and, to some extent, to the physical and economic well-being of the national populations. They pioneered the public service concept of the university and the scientific research function of the university.

There was a potentially more explosive *theoretical* side

of the Enlightenment, however—the reinterpretation through rationalist analysis of basic preconceptions in philosophy, religion, politics, and social relations. Here, the universities were silent. As agencies of the status quo they depended on the community and the government for their continued existence. They could scarcely be expected to lead the way in reconstructing the social order. Voltaire, Diderot, Hume, Montesquieu, Gibbon, and Rousseau were not university teachers. The governments of the "enlightened despots" visualized enlightened higher learning only in narrow terms—as technical and vocational training that would prepare people to make a contribution to the administration and economy of the state.[45]

As the system of public service training at Halle, Göttingen, and Vienna developed, it became clear that, whatever the ideals professed, the reality was thoroughly undemocratic. Students who lacked the necessary social connections or financial resources were effectively shut out from professional competition. They lacked the funds to serve long periods of time as unpaid trainees and therefore had to settle for the less glamorous careers of rural clergyman or secondary school teacher.[46] Leo Gershoy observes: "For all the stimulus Halle and Göttingen supplied to creative scholarship and academic freedom, the temper of higher learning remained singularly lacking in the critical ferment that marked French speculation. . . . Students and professors discharged their obligations without imagination and without raising the question of the validity of those institutional relations that made professional careers possible for them."[47]

Higher learning in 1789 was still a long way from coming to terms with the modern world and thus realizing its full potential. Changes were under way, however, foreshadowing developments of immense significance. Universities were beginning to broaden their concepts of a proper curriculum and to diversify course offerings. They were cautiously coping with the scientific revolution. Most important of all, they were beginning to modify the essential concept of their mission. In an age of the national state, science, and the Enlightenment, universities were no longer solely concerned with the *preservation* and *transmission* of accepted knowledge; they were becoming involved in the *discovery* and *advancement* of new knowledge as well.

5

The University in the Industrial Age: 1789–1914

*T*he French Revolution, with its immense political and social consequences, demarcated the boundaries between the traditional order and a dramatic new era in human history. European universities, along with many other institutions of the Old Regime, underwent fundamental changes after 1789. The combined impact of nationalism, secularism, democracy, technology, and science in the century that followed the great revolution was bound to transform the structure of western higher education in profoundly significant ways.

The State and the Higher Learning

In many nineteenth-century European nations, the role played by the state in higher education became more pronounced. The needs of the state for university-trained personnel to serve the complex social order that had appeared increased measurably as the century progressed.

Problems in fields such as "public health, social services, universal state education, and sometimes nationalized industries," notes M. S. Anderson, "generated a multitude of officials and inspectors."[1]

In this connection, France represents the classic case of a modern, tightly controlled, highly centralized state system of higher education. The Revolution destroyed the traditional university as it had existed since the late middle ages. In its place, a group of utilitarian professional schools and separate liberal arts faculties sprang up. Revolutionary leaders like Robespierre detested the traditional universities as moribund, church-dominated corporations, reactionary in outlook and ignorant of modern science and scholarship. Accordingly, in 1793 the revolutionary authorities abolished all twenty-two French universities and confiscated their endowments, which were henceforth reserved for "the people." Ultimately the very concept of a university encompassing the whole range of human knowledge was dropped, to be replaced by specialized training in a number of specific subjects. The former university faculties became independent, fragmented, nonresidential single-purpose schools.

Examples of the new specialized schools established by the National Convention were a School of Public Works (later the famous École Polytechnique); a School of Oriental Languages; an École Normale to train teachers; and a National Institute for eminent scholars and savants. The preoccupations of war, however, together with runaway inflation, political factionalism, and insufficient funds, prevented many of these proposals from ever becoming more than paper projects. It remained for Napoleon Bonaparte to transform these revolutionary blueprints into functioning institutions.[2]

Terry Nicholas Clark sees the Napoleonic structure as a mixture of an ecclesiastical control of ideas, government

bureaucracy, and the military style of the Emperor."[3]
Under the Ministry of Education, *recteurs* were put in
charge of all the main faculties of higher education in
France. In 1808 the imperial University of France was
given a monopoly over all public instruction in the country, including all separate faculties of theology, law,
medicine, science, and letters. The Napoleonic "university" was intended to train for state service citizens loyal to
their prince, fatherland, and family.[4] Standardized cloth-
ing was obligatory for teachers at all levels, with ranks
distinguished by insignia and military-style epaulettes.[5]

The University system was an extreme example of
centralized control of higher education by an all-powerful
state bureaucracy. In theory, private individuals and
groups still had the right to establish and maintain their
own schools, but in practice the state retained dominance
because it alone had the right to authorize the granting of
all degrees. Nor was its favor given to teachers who dared
to criticize it. Under Napoleon III, for example, professors
such as the historian Michelet, and Mickiewicz, a Slavonic
scholar, were dismissed because they were deemed to be
unfriendly to the regime.[6]

According to a famous but possibly apocryphal story,
a minister of education under the Second Empire pulled
out his watch and exclaimed: "At this very time, in such a
class, all the scholars of the Empire are studying a certain
page in Vergil!" There is a good deal of truth in the tale.
The Napoleonic heritage was incredibly mechanistic and
bureaucratic, yet it displayed enormous staying power.
Writing in 1934, Stephen d'Irsay observed that
Bonaparte's Université de France persisted, substantially
unmodified, for more than a century as the principal
framework for French higher education. "It prevailed
throughout the Restoration," he noted, "the July Monar-

chy, the Second Empire, and the Third Republic, and in form at least it still exists today."[7]

In various German states, where considerable state supervision of universities had existed since Reformation times, the system was now tightened and made more thorough. Ironically, the very reforms initiated by Wilhelm von Humboldt and others of his Enlightenment-minded generation in the early nineteenth century served only to increase the power of the state over higher learning. Humboldt was devoted to the idea of self-expression and personal freedom for university scholars; to this end, he desired that the institution he had founded, the University of Berlin, should have its own independent revenues as a guarantee of autonomy. He further wished that professors be paid generously so that they could concentrate without economic harassment on their main goal of advancing knowledge. However, Humboldt's successors as Prussian ministers of education did not share these ambitions. One of them, von Schuckmann, brusquely set aside any idea of fiscal autonomy for the University of Berlin, stating that universities must not be permitted to become "states within the state." Another minister, von Altenstein, made it clear that university professors on the public payroll had no right to express independent opinions on political matters. It soon became apparent that the budget of the University of Berlin was going to be far smaller than the government had originally promised. Clearly, Humboldt and his colleagues had miscalculated when they thought that their goal of *Wissenschaft* (advancement of learning through disinterested scholarship) and improvement of the moral tone of society could be realized under the control of a bureaucratic state.[8]

As E. J. Hahn points out, the German university of the nineteenth century "was a *self-administering,* but not a *self-governing* corporation.[9] And the ones who played the crucial part in the institution's self-administration were the small minority of senior professors. The junior faculty—*Extra-ordinarinen* (associates) and *Privatdozenten* (unpaid lecturers)—had no voice in the university structure. The senior faculty every year elected the university officials from their own ranks—the rector, the faculty deans, and the members of the University Senate. But more important was the fact that the minister of education, representing the state, retained the real power. After the Karlsbad Decrees of 1819, this official had agents in each university to report to him directly. No rector or dean could serve until he had been confirmed by the minister, after which the university was governed strictly in accordance with the latter's instructions. The only appointment the senior faculty could bestow independently was that of *Privatdozent* (unpaid lecturer). All appointments of professorial grade, associate or senior, were made by the minister, who also controlled all promotions. Since there was no established pay scale, professors bargained individually with the minister on salary matters.[10]

State control was also statutorily rigorous in the universities of the Austro-Hungarian empire. William Johnston notes: "University professors were themselves bureaucrats, personal servants of the emperor, who could veto any appointment."[11] Under the repressive regime of Metternich, before 1848 the Austrian state kept a tight rein on all schools. According to a newspaper account, Emperor Francis told the teachers at the Laibach Lyceum in 1821: "I do not need savants, but good, honest citizens. Your task is to bring young men up to be that. He who serves me must teach what I order him."[12] Under this system, university professors as well as *gymnasium* teachers were to follow a strict routine and to employ only state-permitted texts. Professors and students were watched over closely by police spies and state-appointed directors of studies. Independent thought was discouraged. The result was that even the famous medical school at the University of Vienna went into a decline, its faculty hamstrung by petty restrictions imposed by the Emperor's personal physician, von Stift. One medical treatise was banned because of a passing reference criticizing the roads in Carinthia.[13]

Nationalism in the Universities

"The French Revolution," writes Ferderick B. Artz, "awakened among many of the European peoples a new sense of national solidarity and a new hope for a better national future."[14] This nationalistic spirit increasingly politicized the universities. No longer resembling the international scholarly communities of medieval times, these schools often became the headquarters of national liberation movements.

The classic early nineteenth-century example of nationalistic agitation in universities occurred in Germany. The political disturbances of the French revolutionary period had destroyed a number of German universities. After the battle of Jena, Prussia lay prostrate at the feet of Napoleon, and Halle University was temporarily suppressed. At this low point in national fortune, a movement for "liberation" began with university students in the forefront.

To spread the nationalist gospel, new types of student organizations were required. Until this time, student life at German universities had been dominated by the hard-drinking, dueling fraternities, the *Landsmannschaften,* with their elaborate ritualism and aristocratic exclusiveness. But "Father" Friedrich Ludwig Jahn's new sports associations for youth (the *Turngemeinden)* were designed to be different. They stressed the theme of national unity and avoided caste distinctions. To this end, "Turners" all wore simple grey shirts. Very soon, though, they began to express anti-Semitic or anti-Slavic attitudes and to invade university classrooms to disrupt the lectures of professors labeled "antinational." Soon more permanent nationalistic associations, the *Burschenschaften,* emerged among the students at most German universities, following in the footsteps of the grey shirts. K. H. Jarausch observes that the *Burschenschaften* thus did not really break with the feudalistic past. Many of the former *Landsmannschaftler* became founding fathers of the new *Burschenschaft* chapters and injected into these organizations the sectarian, Teutonic, anti-Semitic, and romanticist prejudices that "colored their life-style."[15]

Some of the activities of the young *Burschenschafter* seemed to anticipate the Nazi tactics in the twentieth century. At a great student assembly held at the Wartburg, near Eisenach, in October 1817, a group of Jahn's followers made a pile of the writings of alleged antinationalists and burned them in a huge public bonfire. Then at the general *Burschentag* held in October 1818, it was proposed to limit membership in the student societies to Christians and Germans only. After lengthy debate, a resolution was adopted defining the goal of the *Allemeine deutsche Burschenschaft* as "Christian-German development by every spiritual and physical force for the service of the fatherland."[16]

In March 1819, Karl Sand, a fanatical follower of the *Schwarz* or *Unbedingte* (unconditional) student extremists, assassinated a conservative writer, August von Kotzebue. This event led to the enactment of the Karlsbad Decrees (September 1819), which were sponsored by the conservative Austrian premier, Prince Metternich. These measures dissolved the *Burschenschaften*, established close supervision of universities throughout the German Confederation, and imposed rigid censorship on all student publications and meetings. A minority of *Burschenschafters* then went underground and continued their crusade as sometimes violent nationalist conspirators.[17]

University Radicalism

Nineteenth-century student activists were often radicals as well as nationalists. They frequently added demands for liberalization and social revolution to their lists of grievances. In time, the authorities came to consider radicalism in the universities even more dangerous to the state than nationalism. For the first time in history, groups in the universities were organizing movements that openly sought to overthrow existing governments.

University radicalism had not been a factor during the French revolution of 1789. If anything, the universities of that day were regarded by the revolutionary authorities as potential centers of *counterrevolutionary* activity. It was not until the Metternich period, the era of political reaction that followed the defeat of Napoleon, that radicalism appeared at certain European universities. In western Europe and Great Britain, where liberal and parliamentary governments provided an outlet for public opinion, unrest was minimal. But in countries that retained a more authoritarian structure, such as Germany, Austria-Hungary, and Russia, student agitation became a serious problem.

Fueling the rising discontent in such countries was the fact that university-trained people were finding it increasingly hard to secure professional positions. The universities were turning out an excessive number of highly trained young academics and professionals. Great Britain, then the most highly industrialized nation, was able to provide careers in business and in the colonial service as alternatives to academic or professional employment, but on the Continent vocational opportunities were fewer and members of the "university-trained proletariat" might, in their very desperation, seek to change the system radically.[18]

In France, rumblings of discontent came occasionally from the nation's engineering school, the École Polytechnique. During the early years of the nineteenth century, Auguste Comte and Michel Chevalier were students there, and it came to be known as "a seminary of Saint-Simonians" (utopian socialists). During the Bourbon Restoration and the July Monarchy, the students opposed the government, and the Polytechnique was closed by the authorities at least four times. Polytechnique students played an active part in the revolutions of 1830 and 1848. In the later nineteenth century, however, radicalism among the "Polytechniciens" subsided.[19]

In Germany, the effort by a small student group to overthrow the confederation government in the 1833 Frankfurt *putsch* was easily suppressed.[20] Many students thereupon turned to more moderate and open forms of political protest, and the growing strength of liberalism among German academics was demonstrated dramatically by the "Göttingen Seven." In 1837, a number of eminent scholars at the University of Göttingen refused to take the required oath of loyalty to the Crown because Ernest Augustus, the sovereign, had revoked the Hanoverian constitution. All seven were dismissed from their positions, but they were hailed as heroes by sympathizers throughout Germany and eventually found jobs in other universities.[21]

The student of the 1840s was more serious than his predecessors and more knowledgeable in politics. His parents, who might be merchants, were usually not part of the bureaucratic power elite. He was therefore much more likely than the *Burschenschafters* of earlier times to challenge the caste system in the state bureaucracy. And he was customarily a "progressive" on internal university matters, opposing the aristocratic *Landsmannschaften*, with their drinking-club ethics and concepts of dueling honor.[22]

As revolutionary fervor swept Europe in 1848, progressive-minded students were in the forefront of the uprisings. They were active in the Munich revolution that forced King Ludwig to abdicate. They were prominent that same year in the outbreaks that temporarily won Berlin for the liberal cause. Indeed, members of the junior faculty at Berlin University were so aroused by the seeming certainty of a progressive triumph that they were emboldened to make a public appeal for a more active role in academic government. Meanwhile in Hesse, students at the University of Giessen made an armed attack on government troops, and at the University of Vienna, students and radical professors formed an Academic Legion of five thousand that erected barricades around the university grounds. When the authorities sought to disband this force, a revolution broke out in the Austrian capital. The student legionnaries eventually secured arms from a state arsenal, drove Prince Metternich from the city, and forced the royal court to flee.[23]

For a while the tide seemed irresistible, but in the end the successes of the academic revolutionists proved to be short-lived. In time, the Prussian army returned to Berlin and restored absolutism with its bayonets. An army loyal to the Hapsburgs reconquered Vienna and suppressed the revolution in the outlying provinces. The Russians crushed the Hungarian liberal regime. Everywhere, by 1849, the counterrevolution was triumphant. Why had the "revolution of the intellectuals" failed so miserably? In part, the failure was due to the inexperience and obvious disorganization of the university revolutionists. In part it was due to serious divisions that developed in their ranks—splits between students and professors, between moderates and radicals, and between one nationality group and another. Finally, and perhaps most important, the revolutionary intellectuals failed to win support from the peasant masses or the urban working classes.

With the collapse of the high hopes of 1848, university radicalism died out in central Europe.[24] In one country—Russia—it continued unabated, however. There, student opponents of the tsar's regime mounted the most violent and sustained university-based protest of the whole nineteenth century. Like Germany and Austria, Russia possessed a rootless and dissatisfied intellectual elite. By 1880 the composition of the student body in Russian universities was changing significantly. Previously these schools had been the preserve mainly of the sons of big landowners, army officers, and high-ranking government bureaucrats. But now many *raznochintsy* (men of no rank) were enrolling in the universities. Their fathers very often were small merchants, artisans, priests, or even in a few instances, peasants. Russia was changing rapidly with the growth of cities and industry, and it needed greater numbers of trained professionals. The regime, however, remained backward and autocratic. The new university-trained elite could not easily secure suitable positions under the autocratic system. The result was that, unlike the aristocratic students of earlier days, the *raznochintsy* became openly hostile to the system. The very word "intelligentsia" came in Russia to signify opposition to the regime.[25]

Under Tsar Nicholas I (1825–1855) the universities were regarded as nothing more than vehicles for training government officials. The watchwords of Nicholas's system were: orthodoxy, autocracy, and nationality. By the 1860s, however, Russian universities were emerging as centers of a very different kind of activity. Riots erupted, political demonstrations were staged, and assassination plots were hatched. Predictably, the tsar's ministers responded with repression—expulsion, arrest, deportation to Siberia. However, these policies were still not harsh enough or consistent enough to stamp out the growing conflagration. Young Russians were permitted to study at foreign universities and later to return to their native land with the "subversive" ideas they had picked up abroad. At one point the desperate Russian authorities banned all philosophy lectures at the universities and decreed that logic could be taught only by professors of theology. Even so, unsettling ideas kept filtering in, and Seton-Watson asserts that "a majority of educated people in Russia were against the regime."[26]

Repression seemed to breed only more opposition. As Nicholas Hans puts it: "The struggle became a vicious circle: the students revolted against the repression, the Government quelled their opposition, arrested and banished thousands of students, but new recruits filled the ranks and the movement would break out again with new force. The universities became the focus of a political struggle against the autocracy and lost their purely academic significance. Thousands of young lives were ruined, national resources and energy were spent without effect in this struggle, but the Government stubbornly continued the policy of repression."[27]

The government of Tsar Alexander II responded to student riots at St. Petersburg and Moscow in 1861 and 1862 by attempting conciliation. A new university statute was issued in 1863 granting a large measure of autonomy to the universities and their staffs. Restlessness and rebelliousness continued, however, and in April 1866 a university student tried to assassinate the tsar. That attempt failed, but in 1881 Alexander was finally killed by a radical terrorist. As new university disturbances swept the country, the government promulgated a tough new university code. This decree took away all forms of autonomy or self-government from Russian institutions of higher learning and banned all student organizations. University students were henceforth to be closely supervised by a government inspector as well as by the police. The number of Jews to be admitted was to be limited to a quota of 10 percent. University fees were to be sharply raised to discourage poorer students from attending.[28]

In spite of these measures (or perhaps because of them) unrest in Russian universities grew even more severe, and by the 1890s thousands of students were being arrested. When a new tsar, Nicholas II, ascended the throne in 1896, he made it clear that he would reject all proposals for liberalization of the country. This fanned student discontent to an even higher pitch. In Moscow, university students formed a union council (*soyuzny soviet*) to defend their interests in confrontations with the authorities and to oppose the government's policies. Soon *soviets* were springing up at other Russian universities. Allegations of police brutality led to a new wave of student strikes and Marxism began to attract a substantial following. As the riots mounted in fury, thousands of students were expelled or arrested and a few were killed. When the revolution of 1905 swept across the country, the universities were in the forefront, the "furnaces of the revolution." Academic work ground to a halt. The tsarist government was finally obliged to yield, and the universities recovered their lost autonomy. For a time, student political agitation subsided. By 1908, however, it was reviving once more as the authorities sought to withdraw the liberal concessions they had been forced to make three years earlier. Eventually, as signs of the coming of World War I developed, the government had to backtrack once more. A liberal education minister, Count Ignatiev, reversed earlier reactionary policies *circa* 1914–16. By this time, however, the collapse of tsardom was not too far distant.[29]

The Advance of Secularism

As the modern state developed and assumed ever larger spheres of power, it circumscribed the authority of organized religion. This inexorable trend toward secularism was closely related to the rise of a complex industrial-urban civilization and the growing intellectual influence of natural science. Liberals like Count Cavour in Italy began to call for "a free church in a free state" while radical anticlericals like Gambetta in France exclaimed: "Clericalism—there is the enemy!" Many countries were agitated by bitter struggles between defenders of the churches and their secularist critics. In this ideological war, the universities of Europe played a crucial role.

In France, the Roman Catholic church and its partisans fought for decades against Napoleon's secular, state-controlled Université de France. Catholic spokesmen denounced it as a state monopoly. The Restoration government sympathized with the Catholic position but was afraid to overthrow Napoleon's creation entirely. While liberals such as Guizot and Cousin were suspended from professorships and the École Normale was suppressed for a time, the royalist *Ultras* attacked the Université structure only in a piecemeal fashion. In 1850, the Comte de Falloux proposed a law that gave ecclesiastics a larger voice in the administration of public education and gave the church, or private individuals for that matter, the right to freely establish secondary schools. However, the *Loi Falloux* left the field of higher education still solely under the control of the Université de France. Even so, the French "left" denounced the measure, and anticlericalism revived notably during the years that followed.[30]

Under monarchist influence, the French assembly rushed through a bill in July 1875 to establish "complete freedom of higher education." The aim was to enable Catholics to set up their own higher faculties, and that church now hastily founded universities at Paris, Lille, Angers, Lyons, and Toulouse, seeking to accomplish this task before the new and possibly secular constitution of the Third Republic went into effect. The republicans and anticlericals were not completely defeated, however. When they regained political power in 1880, they withdrew the right of the new Catholic institutions to award degrees; Only the Université de France retained that right.[31]

Secularism also gathered momentum in nineteenth-century Britain. Ever since the Reformation, England's two oldest universities had been closed to one-half of the nation's population. They were essentially training-places for the Anglican clergy. At Oxford, no one could even matriculate without subscribing to the Thirty-nine Articles of the Church of England. At Cambridge one could not secure a degree, or a university scholarship or fellowship, without doing so. A bill to remove these restrictions was hotly debated in Parliament in 1834. Anglican spokesmen denounced it as an attack on religion itself. The bill was passed by the House of Commons, but was thrown out by the House of Lords. Politicians such as Peel and Melbourne found the issue too hot to handle. For many years they avoided taking a stand on it for fear of alienating important voting blocs.[32]

Meanwhile an independent step was taken toward

the establishment of a more secular university in Britain. After a visit to Germany in 1820, the poet Thomas Campbell proposed that a new university be established in London. A coalition of anti-Tories, liberal nonconformists, and secularists supported the project; prominent personalities such as Macaulay, Grote, Bentham, Mill, and Brougham endorsed it. Soon a "public utility" corporation was founded to raise money for the proposed university. The churches and their partisans, however, together with friends of the older universities, attacked the proposal as one that would create a "radical infidel College, a humbug joint-stock subscription school for Cockney boys, . . . got up in the bubble season." Despite the virulence of the opposition, University College, London, managed to open for instruction in 1828. It was the first purely secular institution of higher education in British history. Nonconformists and even freethinkers were admitted without restrictions, and the school's course of study emphasized science, history, and other purely secular subjects.[33]

The opponents of University College gained a temporary victory, however, when they denied authority to the new school to award degrees. Meanwhile, a staunchly Anglican foundation, King's College, was set up in London to compete with University College. A Tory columnist crowed: "The finishing blow has been given to the stye of infidelity building at the end of Gower Street." But King's College did not prosper in the way its sponsors had hoped and, distasteful as it must have been, an accommodation finally had to be worked out with its rival. The two colleges were joined in a single incorporation known as the University of London, and this new institution was given the power to hold certifying examinations and grant degrees. In 1850 the university was authorized to accept affiliated institutions other than its original two colleges, and in 1858 it was permitted to administer its examinations to persons from all parts of the country. By this time, London University had shown that a predominately non-sectarian university could survive and prosper in England. Its example was most influential some years later in shaping the character of the civic, or "redbrick," universities.[34]

Meanwhile, a movement to reform Oxford and Cambridge gathered strength. Secularists and militant Nonconformists were joined in this endeavor by liberal Anglicans who opposed religious tests on principle. The government entered the picture in 1850 by creating two royal commissions to investigate the universities. Conservative dons denounced this move as "parliamentary interference" and refused to cooperate. The investigators proceeded with their inquiries nevertheless and ultimately recommended the abolition of religious tests. After hot debate, the Whig-Peelite government (with the help of William E. Gladstone) got Parliament to pass the Oxford Act in 1854, which, with a subsequent bill in 1856, put into law the main recommendations of the commissioners. Matriculation and admission to degrees at both universities were now freed from all religious requirements (the church party was still strong enough to retain the policy of excluding non-Anglicans from university fellowships and college offices). This legislation proved to be the turning point. The principle of parliamentary "interference" with the universities had now been established, and broader legislation could not long be delayed. From 1863 onward, bills were introduced almost every year to abolish all remaining religious restrictions. Finally, in 1871, the Tests Act was put through by Gladstone's cabinet. This important bill threw open to non-Anglicans all university offices in Oxford and Cambridge. After that, it was inevitable that Parliament would some day abolish all restrictions on the appointment of college fellows or principals; This was done in 1877. A revolution of sorts had occurred at Oxford and Cambridge.[35]

Popularization of Higher Education

In the years preceeding 1914, higher education for the masses was not yet a reality in Europe. In most countries a two-track system prevailed. One group took the route that led ultimately to the university, while a much larger group followed the path that prepared for business or industrial employment by means of trade school and apprenticeship training. At the same time, industrialization and urbanization were making the masses a more influential factor than ever before in the social and political order. Universities in countries such as Holland, Scotland, and Switzerland began to respond to this phenomenon by seeking to broaden the opportunities for higher education that were available to common people, but other nations moved more slowly in this direction.

In Holland, the government encouraged the expansion of higher education by reorganizing the Amsterdam Athenaeum and converting it into a full-fledged university; in the years following 1876, the new school emerged as the Municipal University of Amsterdam.[36] In Scotland, the universities already possessed the reputation of providing learning for the common people. Instead of a two-track system, says A. Victor Murray, there was "no block in the way of the child of the village working his way up to the university."[37] Fees were low and lodging was far less expensive than in Oxford or Cambridge. It cost approximately £200 a year to attend Cambridge in 1900, but the average charge at the University of Glasgow was £17 (and most of the Scottish students lived at home, so their other expenses were quite modest). Students in the Scottish institutions, Paul L. Robertson points out, "were drawn from a wider field and included many more boys of poorer families" than was true at Oxford and Cambridge.[38]

In Germany the pattern was markedly different. By the 1850s Prussian higher education had become so expensive that the percentage of students from lower-middle-class homes was declining noticeably. Scholarships for poorer students, asserts John Gillis, "were virtually non-existent."[39] Even the rigidly classicist university entrance requirements, according to Fritz Ringer, "were gradually routinized and transformed into defenses of social privilege."[40] The cost of a higher education in Germany by 1885 ranged from four thousand to eight thousand marks, while the yearly salary of a primary school teacher averaged only fifteen-hundred marks. In that year, 7.5 million attended the German primary schools, 238,000 were at the secondary schools, and a mere 27,000 were in attendance at all the universities of Germany. In this context we can better understand this statement by the eminent German sociologist, Max Weber: "Differences of education are one of the strongest . . . social barriers, especially in Germany, where almost all privileged positions inside and outside the civil service are tied to qualifications involving not only specialized knowledge but also 'general cultivation.' "[41]

In England, Oxford and Cambridge maintained their aristocratic character through most of the nineteenth century. Higher education could not serve as broad a constituency as in Scotland or in North America as long as the costly residential and tutorial system of Oxford and Cambridge remained the norm. The English government did little to change the situation.

In time, private initiative tried to do what the state did not do. The Chartist radicals during the 1840s had demanded that children of the working class be admitted to Oxford and Cambridge. While nothing was done to accommodate these desires, the founding of University College (later London University) did help set in motion a movement that was important for the future of democratic higher education in Britain. The new university's charter provided that colleges in the provinces might send their students to take University of London certifying examinations. Candidates who passed these exams qualified for University of London degrees. This provision led to the founding of a number of civic, or "redbrick," universities, such as Owens College in Manchester and Mason College in Birmingham. By 1884 the new university colleges that had sprung up at Manchester, Leeds, and Liverpool decided to combine their forces in order to form one stronger institution, Victoria University. This union did not last long, however; in 1903 the constituent colleges decided to separate once more. At this point, all three institutions received university charters. A year later a University of Sheffield was chartered, and in 1909 a University of Bristol made its debut. Six other university colleges outside of London were founded by 1914—Nottingham, Newcastle, Reading, Exeter, Southampton, and Manchester School of Technology. Meanwhile, London University had been looking to its own laurels and was serving an ever wider constituency. By 1909 it boasted ten affiliated medical schools, six theological colleges, the London School of Economics, an agricultural college, and the Central Technical College of the City of London.[42]

London University and the new civic universities represented a breakthrough in English higher education. They shattered the Oxford-Cambridge monopoly and brought higher learning to the mass of the British people. Of course, they lacked the traditions and financial resources of the older universities and their buildings were uglier—"early Etruscan," said one critic. They were often located in the most run-down areas of industrial cities and their students, mostly commuters, had little chance for a stimulating social life. Then, too, townspeople were sometimes indifferent or even hostile to the "redbricks." D. H. Lawrence, who attended Nottingham College between

1906 and 1908, recalled that the local population seemed to resent the institution, and in his opinion it was "nothing more than a little slovenly laboratory for the factory."[43]

With the rise of the "redbricks," two English university traditions confronted each other. One, the Oxford-Cambridge axis, was closely connected with the national elites of politics, business, the professions, and government. The other, London and the "redbricks," was municipal or provincial and utilitarian, taking its students mainly from nearby localities and giving them a chance to train for middle-class careers. Of the two, only the Oxford-Cambridge tradition had status. As late as 1914 its tutorial-type instruction was regarded as being of superior quality, and its graduates held most of the country's prestigious positions.[44]

A few influential persons at Oxford and Cambridge were aware of the excessively insulated position of their institutions and were anxious to reach out to broader segments of the British public. As early as 1858 Oxford and Cambridge agreed to administer local examinations to certify the quality of work being done in the various mechanics institutes. About the same time, the two universities began to offer special lectures for "adult popular audiences." The next step came in 1867, when James Stuart, a Cambridge don, began his own personal program of "university extension" by lecturing (usually on Astronomy) in the industrial towns of north England, reaching large audiences of working-class people. Stuart had great success, and in 1873 the Cambridge authorities accepted his program, establishing a University Extension division.[45]

By the 1890s both Oxford and Cambridge had flourishing University Extension programs going. Some of their best professors were sent to lecture far from the university halls on subjects such as Greek art, the French

Revolution, Shakespeare, and the Italian Renaissance. More than fifty thousand people a year were reached by this program during the 1890s, the majority of them adults. The program contributed to the enlargement of Yorkshire College and the establishment of new colleges at Bristol, Sheffield, and Nottingham. It led to the establishment of two new "Extension Colleges" at Reading and Exeter, which sought to link extension teaching with the improvement of the secondary schools. Meanwhile, traveling libraries were set up as an adjunct to the lecture programs and summer session courses were offered for the first time. Then, in 1899, the trade union movement appeared on the academic scene and established a college in the heart of Oxford. This was Ruskin College, a school specifically designed to train trade union leaders.[46]

Higher Education for Women

Nineteenth-century European universities began to include significant numbers of women in their expanded constituencies. Little was done in the early decades of the century, but as a result of the growing women's rights movements, the universities came under increased pressure after 1850 to do something for women. Some of the institutions generously admitted women to their courses, but others provided such privileges only "grudgingly and on a very inadequate scale," reports M. S. Anderson.[47]

Sidney Webb states that the University of Zurich was the first in Europe to offer university-level courses to women. This happened in 1867; and by 1892 women were themselves permitted to lecture at the Swiss institution.[48] Also in the late 1860s, the university faculty at Paris decided to admit women; by 1909 some thirty-five hundred young women were enrolled in French university programs.[49] Universities in other countries admitted women in the following order: Swedish and Finnish, 1870; Danish, 1875; Italian, 1876; Norwegian, 1884; Spanish and Rumanian, 1888; Belgian and Greek, 1890; and Scottish, 1892. Once the movement for women's higher education started, it seemed to snowball.[50]

The women's cause made surprising progress even in Russia, a country that remained in so many respects backward and autocratic. As early as 1858 special *gymnasia* for girls were established there. By 1873, at least 190 secondary schools for girls were operating in the country. However, when the Russian Ministry of Public Instruction polled the universities in 1861 on the question of admitting women, it encountered such strong opposition from the universities of Moscow and Dorpat that it dropped the idea. The Russian university statute of 1863 unequivocally barred women. Soon thereafter, Russian young women seeking a higher education began to go abroad. A number of them enrolled at the University of Zurich, reports Nicholas Hans, forming an important part of "the first body of women students in Europe."[51]

In the years that followed, the Russian government blew hot and cold on the question of women's higher education. In 1872, Moscow University introduced "higher courses" for women, and other universities followed suit. However, in the more reactionary mood of the late 1880s the government closed down nearly all these courses. In the 1890s, the restrictions were lifted once again. In 1897, the Medical Institute for Women in St. Petersburg reopened as a university-level institution, and soon one thousand students enrolled there. In 1900, "higher courses" for women in Moscow received a state subsidy. By 1903 an institution of higher education for women had opened in Odessa. Subsequently, as a result of the liberalization that followed the revolution of 1905, women's "higher courses" were established in nearly every state-supported Russian university. At the same time, many privately financed programs for women were developed. By 1910, twenty thousand Russian women were enrolled in university-level courses out of a total of approximately ninety thousand students.[52]

Opportunities for higher training were much less favorable for German women. Gordon Craig characterizes the condition of women in nineteenth-century German society as "truly deplorable." Denied basic civil rights, they could neither vote nor be members of political organizations and trade unions. As early as 1872 an Association for the Higher Education of Women appeared in Germany, but it made little progress. In Prussia it was not until 1896 that girls were permitted to take the examinations for the *Reifezeugnis,* the certificate testifying to the completion of a *gymnasium* education. More and more German states during the 1890s began to throw open their previously all-male secondary schools to girls, but it wasn't until 1908 that girls were admitted to the special secondary-school programs that led to the university. For many years no Prussian universities would admit women; their only female students came from abroad. German young women were obliged to go across the border to Switzerland to obtain a higher education. After 1900, Prussian universities began to admit women, but even then females were not permitted to take the *Staatsexam* that qualified students to secure university degrees. Gradually, women began to enter the universities in ever larger numbers, and by 1914 they constituted about 7 percent of all university students in Prussia.[53]

Conditions for women were even more difficult in Austria-Hungary. They did not gain entry to the University of Vienna until 1897 and then only to the Philosophical Faculty. In 1892 the Medical Faculty at Vienna was temporarily opened to women, but only as the result of a decree by the emperor, which was vehemently opposed by almost the entire university. The dean of the medical faculty wrote one of his colleagues at the time that it was well documented that most women's brains were less fully developed than those of males.[54]

In the universities of England, women made more headway than in Germany or Austria, but the going was not easy. In 1848, an institution of higher education for women, Queen's College, opened in London. In addition, Bedford College, also in London, was officially chartered about this time as an institution of learning for women. And in 1870 University College (part of the University of London) decided to admit women. In 1878 when the University of London became a teaching institution, it began to grant university degrees and to make teaching posts available to women. Women's rights advocates won an important victory in 1875 when Parliament enacted a statute that authorized all newly established universities to confer degrees on women. Under this law, women were admitted to such universities as Victoria, Manchester, Liverpool, Leeds, Sheffield, Bristol, Birmingham, and Wales.[55]

Oxford and Cambridge, though, together with most British medical and law schools, remained "bastions of male privilege." Then in the 1870s, two determined women stormed their gates. In 1869 Emily Davies founded Girton College for women near Cambridge; three years later she moved it to the heart of that university community. Anne Clough established lecture courses for women in Liverpool and was later encouraged by Professor Henry Sidgwick to transfer this program to Cambridge. As a result, in 1874 she established Newnham College there. Eventually Girton College asked that its students be admitted to the lectures at Cambridge University, while

Newnham requested that its students be admitted to Cambridge University examinations. Eventually these requests were granted, and both institutions became members of the Cambridge community. Similar developments produced separate women's colleges at Oxford in the late nineteenth century, and these, too, eventually affiliated themselves with the university. In 1878 Lady Margaret Hall College was founded at Oxford and a year later Somerville College made its debut there. Sir Hugh's became the university's third women's college in 1886, and St. Hilda's, an institution for teacher training, started in 1893.[56]

It was one thing to establish such schools, but a far more difficult proposition to gain acceptance and equal status for them. The Oxford and Cambridge faculties, characterized by Élie Halévy as "two clubs of conservative old bachelors," adamantly refused to admit graduates of the women's colleges to university degrees or to give their faculty members the same recognition as the dons of the male colleges. Some parents voiced anxieties about the immorality that might flourish as a result of coeducation during adolescent years (at first, the women students were only permitted to attend the regular university lectures with a chaperone). Still it was difficult to explain away the fact that in 1887 a Girton student won "highest first class" in the classical *tripos* (honors examination), and in 1890 a Newnham student bested the "senior wrangler" in the highly prized mathematical *tripos*. Such feats silenced talk about the alleged intellectual inferiority of women.[57]

Science and Technology in the Universities

The nineteenth century was an era of dramatic advances in science and technology as well as an age of rapid industrial and urban growth. An explosion of knowledge about the world of nature was taking place that obliged universities to revise their courses of study and to broaden their definitions of academic learning.

Technical schools had existed in France and Germany before the French Revolution, but it wasn't until the 1790s that the first colleges appeared that were concerned exclusively with modern science and industry. During the revolution, writes C. C. Gillespie, France "endowed herself almost at a stroke with a modern set of scientific institutions."[58] Outstanding among these was the *École Polytechnique*, an institution that became the model for most later schools of technology in countries such as Switzerland, Holland, Austria, and Germany. About the same time, the University of Berlin began its operations, becoming the prototype for all research-minded universities later in the nineteenth century.

Even before the *École Polytechnique* made its debut in 1793, eminent scientists such as LaPlace, Monge, and LaGrange had joined the faculty of another new school created by the French Convention, the École normale superieure. This institution, together with the Polytechnique, was designed to replace the pre-1789 universities, which were regarded by the revolutionary regime as hopelessly moribund. Most of France's leading scientists eventually moved over to the École Polytechnique, an amalgam of all the previous royal schools of engineering.[59] Under Napoleon it became paramilitary, and its four-year scientific and mathematical course was narrowed down to suit the purposes of the French armed forces. The great majority of its graduates became engineering officers or technical specialists in the state bureaucracy.

In time, the "Polytechniciens" emerged as an elite among French students. Only the most able boys were admitted, many of them on scholarship. They received instruction from some of the most brilliant intellects of France. By 1905, however, the military orientation of the school was passing. More Polytechniciens were going into private industry than were taking up military careers. They were a key leadership group, notes Theodore Zeldin, that was "the vital link between the French government and the army and industry."[60]

The Napoleonic government saw all higher education, not just the Polytechnique, as essentially utilitarian and closely linked to national interests. New institutions that appeared during the Napoleonic period reflected this emphasis, among them the National Agronomic Institute, the School of Physics and Industrial Chemistry, and the School of Higher Commercial Studies. All the while, the number of advanced students of science in France steadily increased.[61]

During the late 1860s Napoleon III's education minister, Victor Duruy, founded the École Pratique des Hautes Études as a center of research and teaching in mathematics, natural science, and social science. The new school sponsored the researches of a small group of scholars and was the first to introduce the seminar system in France.[62]

Renewed interest in the reform of France's higher faculties developed as a result of the country's defeat by the Prussians in 1870. Ernest Renan declared that it was the German universities that had won the war. At first there was much discussion, but little action. In 1883, Jules Ferry invited professors to send in their opinions about the advisability of amalgamating the existing independent faculties into provincial universities with better research facilities. Discussions dragged on without any consensus, but finally in 1896 the faculties were reunited and seventeen provincial universities made their appearance.[63]

One of the first actions of the new Swiss federal government in 1848 was to found a polytechnic school in

Zurich. This Federal Institute of Technology was strongly influenced by the École Polytechnique in Paris. In turn, the Swiss institution became a model for the Technische Hochschulen (Technical Higher Schools) of Germany and Austria. Like their French and Swiss prototypes, these institutions were concerned primarily with training factory managers and scientist-technologists. Technische Hochschulen were established in Vienna, Berlin, Munich, Augsburg, Hanover, Stuttgart, Karlsruhe, Nuremberg, Darmstadt, Aachen and Brunswick. They made an important contribution to the German Empire's growing industrial prominence. It was not until 1899, however, that they were officially recognized as possessing university status. Meanwhile, in response to demands by the imperial government and the rising industrial and business establishment, research institutions in the applied sciences were set up that were independent of the universities. The best known were the Physikalisch-Technische Reichsenstalt, founded in 1887, and the Kaiser-Wilhelm Gesellschaft, established in 1911.[64]

Science nevertheless came to play an increasingly significant role in the traditional German universities. Theodore Merz, commenting on this trend, observed: "The university system, in one word, not only teaches knowledge, but above all, it teaches *research*. This is its pride and the foundation of its fame."[65] The founding of the University of Berlin in 1808 was the key event that crystallized these new tendencies. It soon became a model for other German institutions of higher education and a stimulus to their expansion. New universities emerged that sought to rival Berlin, notably Bonn and Munich, while older ones, such as Heidelberg, were reorganized.[66] In most of them the new focus on research brought into prominence the twin concepts of *Lernfreiheit* (the freedom of the student to choose his own studies and to live independently of the university) and *Lehrfreiheit* (the freedom of the professor to investigate and to teach, without interference, the findings of his research within his field of scholarly competence).[67] As Charles McClelland notes: "Nineteenth-century scholars in Germany . . . were convinced that the knowledge of their predecessors was superficial at best, and that bold acts of intelligence and will by the single scholar could uncover the profound secrets of the human world and the universe beyond."[68]

In the field of science teaching, the most dramatic expression of the new research orientation was the laboratory. Germany did not invent the modern scientific laboratory; it had already made an appearance in early nineteenth century France at the École Polytechnique and the Museum d'histoire naturelle, and in England at the Royal Institution. What the German university did was to adapt laboratory research to its teaching procedures, making it a key part of a combined research and instructional program leading to the doctorate. The prototype German university laboratory was developed by the noted chemist, Justus Liebig, at Giessen during the 1830s. This was very much a teaching laboratory in which young people were systematically introduced to a thorough knowledge of chemical properties and concepts.[69] The laboratory at Giessen inspired the creation of similar facilities at a number of other German universities, such as Purkinje's pioneering physiological laboratory at Breslau. As a result, most of Germany's outstanding scientists in the nineteenth century—the mathematician, Gauss; the physiologist, Muller; the physicist, Weber; and later Dubois-Reymond, Helmholz, Virchow, and Koch—were members of university faculties.

In the later decades of the century, libraries and research facilities at German universities grew impressively. Government support for the now-dominant research ethic stimulated the organization of dozens of university seminars and an equally large number of university-affiliated institutes (which were the equivalent of seminars for the medical and natural sciences). By this time, students were coming to these universities from all over the world. In the early twentieth century, foreign students constituted nearly 9 percent of the total enrollment in German universities. The contingent from the United States was particularly large, going back as it did to a visit to Göttingen in 1815 by Edward Everett and George Ticknor. Eventually, the graduate schools of America were reconstructed mainly along German lines. Other countries, too, copied important aspects of the German university system, especially Japan, Greece, Holland, Belgium, Russia, Denmark, Norway, and Sweden. Both France and England were impelled by the dramatic success of the German university to undertake substantial reorganizations of their own systems of higher education.[70]

It is ironic that England, the first home of the Industrial Revolution, should have been slow to offer university-level instruction in technology and science. Prior to 1830, notes C. C. Gillispie, "there was as yet no such thing as a scientific profession in England, nor any institutions in which to launch a scientific career."[71] Oxford and Cambridge were still dominated by a classicist orientation and, as a consequence, most of England's talented and creative scientists continued to be nonacademics whose principal training had come through a form of apprenticeship.

During the 1830s, the newly organized British Association for the Advancement of Science waged a vigorous campaign to secure greater academic recognition for the natural sciences. Important recruits were won to the cause. Prominent industrialists in the north of England appreciated the economic advantages of increased science education, and Albert, the Prince Consort, used his influence and prestige to sponsor it wherever he could. The world fairs held during these years, such as the Crystal Palace Exposition and the Paris Exposition of 1867, focused the British public's attention on the subject. Many Englishmen were alarmed when they learned that British products had won only twelve awards at Paris. This led to the fear, Erich Ashby observes, that "despite Britain's long start in the industrial revolution and despite her easy access to raw materials . . . continental countries were overtaking her in some branches of technology."[72]

Because of the conservatism of Oxford and Cambridge, the first steps toward modernizing England's university curriculum came at newer institutions such as London University and the Royal College of Chemistry. Prince Albert, who had come from Germany, was familiar with Liebig's science teaching program at Giessen: the Royal College's curriculum was modeled on it. A. W. von Hofmann was invited over from Germany to develop this pioneer program and to introduce German research methods into Britain.[73]

The most significant response to the challenges of the age, however, came at the new civic, or "redbrick," universities in the provinces. These institutions, located in fast-growing industrial cities, were more vocationally oriented than Oxford and Cambridge and more responsive to the technological and scientific needs of the country.[74] Civic-minded entrepreneurs had provided the funds and supplied the initiative to get these schools started. Such men feared competition from the continent but they were also motivated by "appreciation of the industrial benefits gained by Germany, France, and Switzerland from their polytechnics and admiration of the American land grant colleges."[75]

John Owens, founder of the University of Manchester, had made a fortune as a cotton textile manufacturer.

Mark Firth, a local steelmaster, made important contributions to the University of Sheffield. In 1880, a number of prominent British mine owners endowed the College of Physical Science at Newcastle with Britain's first chair of mining. Soon thereafter, they established another at the University of Birmingham, where a model coal mine was used to give students practice in underground surveying.[76]

With such sponsorship, it was inevitable that the utilitarian emphasis would predominate at the civic universities. The University of Liverpool was the first British educational institution to develop a comprehensive curriculum for training architects. A large endowment provided a chair in engineering at the University of Birmingham; eventually that institution also offered a degree in Commerce. Reading specialized in agricultural science. Bristol maintained the Agricultural and Horticultural Research station at Long Ashton. Leeds sponsored the study of rescue apparatus for mining operations. Indeed, writes A. Victor Murray, "Leeds had a department of dyeing before it had a department of English."[77] In the nation's metropolis, meanwhile, the rapidly expanding University of London had a number of prominent medical schools, hospitals, and scientific institutions affiliated with it. Among these were the Imperial College of Science and Technology and the London School of Economics.[78]

Oxford and Cambridge lagged behind in scientific and technological education. The royal investigating commissions of 1850 reported that Oxford paid "too little attention to the advancement of knowledge." Some halting steps had been taken, however, in the direction of breaking the classical mold. In 1848, Cambridge introduced *triposes* in the natural sciences. In 1850, Oxford founded two new "honors schools," one for the natural sciences and one for law and modern history. Science classes, however, still lacked the prestige of the more traditional courses.[79]

By the 1860s Englishmen who had been at the German universities had founded a Society for the Organization of Academical Study. One of its members was Mark Pattison, a prominent humanist who was rector of Lincoln College, Oxford. During the late 1860s Pattison published two widely discussed essays calling for university reform along German lines. He appealed for more emphasis on research and more cultivation of the scientific attitude of mind. He castigated the current English practice of "treating a university as a mere continuation school for grown-up schoolboys cramming for examinations." Oxonians and Cantabrigians had only to look to Owens College in Manchester (later the University of Manchester) to find an example of the German university system already at work in England. There, H. E. Roscoe and A. W. Ward had introduced German-style research methods. Indeed, Roscoe in 1874 brought a scholar from Germany, Carl Schorlemmer, to fill the first British chair of organic chemistry.[80]

Academic reform at Oxford and Cambridge was prodded forward by the government. The Oxford and Cambridge University Act of 1877 provided that henceforth a certain portion of the revenues received by the colleges was to be used to strengthen and expand offerings in the natural sciences. Entrance requirements in both universities were now made uniform. Undergraduates were authorized to attend lectures freely outside their own colleges. The University fellows were no longer obligated to remain celibate, and a number of new temporary fellowships, unconnected with teaching or administrative duties, were set aside as research appointments. Thus Parliament helped bring the modern age to Oxford and Cambridge. Meanwhile, the two schools had begun to take steps on their own to improve their facilities for scientific research. Between 1855 and 1860, Oxford constructed a number of modern science laboratories, and in 1871 the duke of Devonshire gave Cambridge funds to establish the renowned Cavendish Laboratory. By the 1880s scientific research was flourishing at both places.[81]

Universities on Trial

All in all, the period from the French Revolution to the outbreak of the First World War was an exciting and significant epoch in the history of the universities of Europe. These institutions were caught up in the political turmoil and rapid socioeconomic evolution of the times. An age of industrialization, bureaucratization, and popularization let loose powerful pressures to make higher education more responsive to the demands of society. In many important areas the universities responded positively and creatively to these pressures. Without question, the main direction of university growth by 1914 indicated that a necessary accommodation was developing between the classical university tradition and the realities of an emergent mass-oriented, technological civilization. The full implications of that far-reaching readjustment would be spelled out in the decades that followed.

6

Exporting the University

After four centuries of continuous growth on the European continent, the university spread to lands far from its place of origin. This cultural migration without doubt is one of the most significant developments in the history of the modern world.[1]

The global expansion of European higher education began within fifty years of Christopher Columbus's first voyage, when the Spaniards founded universities in their newly conquered American domains.[2] Following in their footsteps were the English and the French, who established colleges and seminaries in their seventeenth-century settlements fringing the wilderness of North America. By the nineteenth century, the British were setting up additional institutions of higher education in their newer colonial acquisitions of Canada, Australia, and Cape Colony. The models for these overseas institutions were all to be found in Europe—Salamanca for the Spanish ones, Paris for the French, and Oxford, Cambridge, and the Scottish universities for the British. Later, the University of London became another important prototype for

overseas schools in the British Empire and Commonwealth.[3]

In all of this a basic chronology may be discerned.
Most of the earlier establishments of European-derived
universities were designed primarily to serve the needs of
colonists or expatriates who had settled in distant lands.
Some were founded to realize religious aims (as in New
England) or to spread a religious message to non-
Christians (as in Latin America, French Canada,a or the
Philippines). Some were intended to make professional
and ministerial training available to the overseas colonists
that would otherwise only be obtainable in the homeland.
And these overseas foundations also sought to help Europeans administer and govern their colonial possessions
more effectively.[4]

In more recent times, the university movement beyond the confines of Europe has followed a somewhat
different pattern. More and more it has been involved
with efforts to bring European know-how to a wide range
of non-European peoples. Beginning in the nineteenth
century, as a result, European-style universities appeared
for the first time in various non-Western societies where
they competed with, and in some cases even supplanted,
ancient and indigenous centers of learning. Very often,
the non-European governments (as in Japan, the Near
East, and Africa) sponsored such university projects in
order to import Western European science and technology. They hoped to train native technicians in Western
methods so that the resources of their countries might be
developed.[5]

Universities throughout the world duplicated many
of the experiences of their European prototypes. As a case
in point, many overseas institutions experienced a growth
in enrollments ranging from moderate to massive. Higher
education for the masses became a world phenomenon as

industrialization and urbanization spread during the twentieth century. University enrollments in India, for example, mushroomed from 23,000 in 1901 to 225,000 in 1946, and then 2.7 million in 1971.[6] Brazilian enrollments in all branches of higher education totalled 155,000 in 1965 and then suddenly zoomed to 1 million by 1972.[7]

Wherever Western concepts of higher education were implanted, opportunities for learning broadened significantly. Sometimes this trend toward popularization was very modest at first, but inherent in it was massive expansion. In India, as an example, the British introduced for the first time an open-door policy of admission to higher learning, which had revolutionary implications for Indian society. In essence, notes an Indian scholar, this meant that "learning, hitherto mainly confined to Brahmans, rulers, or aristocrats, was now available to all who cared for it. . . ."[8] Throughout the Middle East and Asia, moreover, the coming of the Western-type university meant that women had an opportunity for higher education where none existed before. This was true even in lands that rejected coeducation.[9]

Reactions to the European-derived university varied according to the differing characteristics of the regions to which it was brought. In new and sparsely settled areas of the world such as Canada, Australia, Latin America, and the early United States, the university was viewed as a tool to preserve a much-prized cultural heritage in a frontier environment. By contrast, in more thickly populated areas that already possessed ancient and indigenous cultures (such as India or China) the Western university had to be adapted very carefully to the necessities and outlooks of a thoroughly dissimilar society. Sometimes it was welcomed enthusiastically; sometimes it was vehemently opposed. Underdeveloped nations have looked to the imported university for swift access to modern scientific and technological information. For example, the countries of modern Africa, (Kenya, Nigeria, Ghana, etc.) "have eagerly adopted the European university," notes Eric Ashby, "and are grateful that the models exported to them are the best the metropolitan countries could offer."[10]

While in some instances Western higher education has been employed in some developing countries to realize the aims and the interests of ruling groups, in other nations it has had a revolutionary impact on the power structure. We have already seen that the university emerged from time to time in European history as the political conscience of nations. This has also been true in the Third World. Young people trained in the European-type universities of the Near and Middle East, Africa, and Asia emerged in later years as nationalist leaders. Thus the West imported into these lands an institution that helped prepare the way for a crusade against Western imperialism. Leaders such as Chou En-lai, Jawaharlal Nehru, and Ho Chi Minh, who played decisive roles in the national liberation of India, China, and IndoChina had either studied at universities in Europe or at universities founded by Europeans in their own countries.[11]

Universities have remained for eight hundred years the world's most fruitful nurseries of humanism and science, scholarship and social responsibility. In Europe, their birthplace, and also in Asia, Africa, and the Americas, they have served as vehicles to help humankind realize its highest aspirations. Yet in age after age these institutions of the highest learning have been obliged to grapple with difficulties created by suspicious bureaucracies, political manipulators, ecclesiastical or ideological dogmatists, and myopic utilitarians. The universities have somehow always survived such threats and pressures. In the last analysis, they have remained dedicated to their basic task: to further the quest for truth and to release the full potential of human creativity. This is perhaps the most important theme that emerges from a comprehensive review of university history. Eight centuries after the first faculties were organized at Paris and Bologna, universities continue, despite all obstacles, to guard the world's most precious treasure: "the culture. the system of vital ideas, which the age has attained."[12]

Notes

Preface

1. Eric Ashby, "Ivory Towers in Tomorrow's World," *Journal of Higher Education,* 38 (November 1967): 417.
2. Hans Kohn. *The Twentieth Century: The Challenge to the West and Its Response* (New York: Macmillan Co., 1957), 248.

Chapter 1

1. James Bowen, *A History of Western Education* (New York: St. Martin's Press, 1972), 1:12–41; William Smith, *Ancient Education* (New York: Philosophical Library, 1955), 67–68.
2. Werner Jaeger, *Paideia: The Ideals of Greek Culture* (New York: Oxford University Press, 1945), 1:316–17; Bowen, *History of Western Education* 1:91–92.
3. Edward A. Parsons, *The Alexandrian Library* (New York: American Elsevier Publishing Co., 1952), 273–74; Smith, *Ancient Education,* 147–48; Bowen, *History of Western Education* 1:159–60.
4. Donald L. Clark, *Rhetoric in Greco-Roman Education* (New York: Columbia University Press, 1957), 60–64; Stobart, *The Grandeur That Was Rome* (London: Sidgwick and Jackson, 1961), 258–63; Bowen, *History of Western Education* 1:188–90.
5. Georgina Buckland, "Byzantine Education" in Norman H. Baynes and H. St. L. B. Moss, eds., *Byzantium* (London: Oxford University Press, 1948), 215; J. M. Hussey, *Church and Learning in the Byzantine Empire, 867–1185* (New York: Russell & Russell, 1963), 52–73; Steven Runciman, *The Last Byzantine Renaissance* (Cambridge: Cambridge University Press, 1970), 54.
6. Edwyn Hole *Andalus: Spain Under the Muslims* (London: Robert Hale, 1958), 39–42; Herbert M. J. Loewe, "The Seljugs," in *The Cambridge Medieval History*

(Cambridge: Cambridge University Press, 1927), 4:304–6; A. G. Little, "Scholastic Philosophy and Universities," in Arthur Tilley, *Medieval France* (New York: Hafner Publishing Co., 1964), 225–26.

7. John B. Mullinger, "Universities," in *Encyclopedia Britannica* (eleventh edition, 1911) 17:751.

8. Hastings Rashdall, "The Medieval Universities," in *The Cambridge Medieval History* vol. 6 (Cambridge: Cambridge University Press, 1936), 562.

9. Bowen, *History of Western Education* 1:110–11, 125–27.

10. Christopher Driver, *The Exploding University* (New York: Bobbs-Merrill Co., 1971), 85.

11. Driver, *The Exploding University*, 85–86; Bowen, *History of Western Education* 1:126–27.

12. Bowen, *History of Western Education* 1:128–29.

13. Rashdall, "The Medieval Universities," 569–70.

14. Mullinger, "Universities," 751.

15. John W. Baldwin and Richard A. Goldthwaite, eds., *Universities in Politics* (Baltimore, Md.: Johns Hopkins Press, 1972), 8–12.

16. Rashdall, "Universities," 563–64.

17. Rashdall, "Universities," 565–67.

18. Samuel Eliot Morison, *The Founding of Harvard College,* (Cambridge, Mass.: Harvard University Press, 1935), 12–14; Bowen, *History of Western Education* (New York: St. Martin's Press, 1975),2:233.

19. Morison, *Founding of Harvard College,* 14.

20. Rashdall, "Universities," 566.

21. Pearl Kibre, *Scholarly Privileges in the Middle Ages* (Cambridge, Mass.: Medieval Academy of America, 1962), 2–12.

22. Rashdall, "Universities," 566–67; Morison, *Founding of Harvard College,* 14–15.

23. Baldwin and Goldthwaite, eds., *Universities in Politics,* 11–16; Bowen, *History of Western Education* 1:111–13.

24. Rashdall, "Universities," 570.

25. Robert S. Rait, *Life in the Medieval University* (Cambridge: Cambridge University Press, 1912), 6–9.

26. Stephen d'Irsay, "Universities and Colleges," in *Encyclopedia of the Social Sciences* (New York: Macmillan and Co., 1934), 15:181–82.

27. Morison, *Founding of Harvard College,* 16–17; Rait, *Life in the Medieval University,* 6–7.

28. Bowen, *History of Western Education* 2:271–72.

29. Rashdall, "Universities," 568; Little, "Scholastic Philosophy and Universities," 221–22.

30. Baldwin and Goldthwaite, eds., *Universities in Politics,* 10.

31. Morison, *Founding of Harvard College,* 20.

32. Morison, *Founding of Harvard College,* 33.

33. Harry Elmer Barnes, *An Intellectual and Cultural History of the Western World* (New York: Dover Publications, 1963), 1:410.

34. Louis J. Paetow, *The Arts Course at Medieval Universities* (Urbana,: University of Illinois Press, 1910), 501–2.

35. Hastings Rashdall, *The Universities of Europe in the Middle Ages* (Oxford: Clarendon Press, 1951), 3:444–46.

36. James R. Banker, "The Ars Dictaminis and Rhetorical Textbooks at the Bolognese University in the Fourteenth Century," *Medievalia et Humanistica*, N. S. 5 (1974): 153–63.

37. Morison, *Founding of Harvard College*, 21.

38. Nathan Schachner, *The Medieval Universities* (New York: A. S. Barnes and Co., 1962), 372–75.

39. Morison, *Founding of Harvard College*, 24.

40. Bowen, *History of Western Education* 1:118.

41. Morison, *Founding of Harvard College*, 24–25; Wallace Notestein, *The English People on the Eve of Colonization, 1603–1630* (New York: Harper & Row, 1954), 133–34.

42. Johann Huizinga, *Erasmus and the Age of the Reformation* (New York: Harper & Row, 1957), 20.

43. Morison, *Founding of Harvard College*, 38.

44. Joseph Ben-David, "Universities," *Encyclopedia of the Social Sciences*, (New York: The Free Press, 1968), 16:192.

45. Stephen d'Irsay, *Histoire des Universités Francaise et étrangères* (Paris: Auguste Picard, 1935), 1:155–57.

46. d'Irsay, "Universities and Colleges," 182; Rait, *Life in the Medieval University*, 147–48.

47. Morison, *Founding of Harvard College*, 18.

48. Joel T. Rosenthal, "The Universities and the Medieval English Nobility," *History of Education Quarterly* 9 (Winter 1969), 433–34.

49. J. W. Adamson, "Education," in F. J. C. Hearnshaw, ed., *Medieval Contributions to Modern Civilization* (London: George G. Harrap, 1921), 208–9.

50. Driver, *The Exploding University*, 91–92.

51. d'Irsay, "Universities and Colleges," 182; Little, "Scholastic Philosophy and Universities," 237.

52. Barnes, *Intellectual History of the Western World* 1:417.

53. Murray G. Ross, *The University: The Anatomy of Academe* (New York: McGraw-Hill, 1976), 8–9.

54. Ben-David, "Universities," 192–93; Little, "Scholastic Philosophy and Universities," 237.

55. Rashdall, *The Universities of Europe* 3:459.

Chapter 2

1. Gene Brucker, *Renaissance Florence* (New York: John Wiley & Sons, 1969), 323.

2. Theodor Klette, *Beiträge zur Geschichte und Literatur der Italienischen Gelehrteurenaissance* (Hildesheim: G. Olms, 1970); Remigio Sabbadini, *Le Scoperte dei Codici Latini e Greci ne' secoli XIV e XV* (Florence: G. C. Sansoni, 1967).

3. Alessandro Gherardi, *Statuti dell'Università e Studio Fiorentino dell 'anno 1387 Seguiti de un appendice di documenti del 1320 al 1472* (Florence: Tipi di M. Cellini, 1881) 1:247–28, as quoted in Brucker, *Renaissance Florence*, 228.

4. *Guidice degli Appelli* 71, pt. 2, Fol. 151–151, 181–182, July 31 and September 29, 1398, as quoted in Brucker, *Renaissance Florence*, p. 227.

5. *Atti del Esecutore degli Ordinamenti della Giustizia* 555 fol. 15, as quoted in Brucker, *Renaissance Florence*, p. 233.

6. Gherardi, *Statuti*, 121–30, 178–81, 413–20, 441–48; as quoted in Brucker, *Renaissance Florence*, 228–35; Lauro Martines. *The Social World of the Florentine Humanists, 1390–1460* (Princeton, N.J.: Princeton University Press, 1963), 313–20; D. Zanetti. "Les salaires des professeurs de L'Université de Pavie," *Annales Economies Sociétés Civilizations* 17 (1962): 426–30.

7. Stephen d'Irsay, *Histoire des Universités francaises et étrangères* (Paris: Auguste Picard, 1935), 1:243–48.

8. Paul Oskar Kristeller, "The Philosophy of Man in the Italian Renaissance," *Italica* (June 1947), 93–112; Robert S. Lopez, *The Three Ages of the Italian Renaissance* (Charlottesville: University of Virginia Press, 1970), 51–52; Alfred Weber and Ralph Barton Perry, *History of Philosophy* (New York: Charles Scribner's Sons, 1896), 214–17.

9. Erasmus of Rotterdam to . . . his friend Thomas Grey, August 1497, in *The Correspondence of Erasmus* trans. R. A. B. Mynors and D. F. S. Thomson (Toronto: University of Toronto Press, 1974), 135–38.

10. Marcel Godet, *La Congrégation de Montaign, 1490–1580* (Paris: H. Champion, 1912), i–vi, 5–33.

11. James N. Overfield, "Scholastic Opposition to Humanism in Pre-Reformation Germany," *Viator, Medieval, and Renaissance, Studies* 7(1976): 400–26; Leopold von Ranke, *History of the Reformation in Germany* (New York: Frederick Ungar, 1966).

12.Terrence Heath, "Logical Grammar, Grammatical Logic, and Humanism in Three German Universities," *Studies in the Renaissance* 18 (1971); Overfield, "Scholastic Opposition to Humanism," 406–9.

13. As quoted in Richard C. Jebb, "The Classical Renaissance," *The Cambridge Modern History* (Cambridge: Cambridge University Press, 1902), 1:543.

14. Douglas Radcliff-Umstead, "The Italian University as Drama" in *The University World, A Synoptic View of Higher Education* (Pittsburgh: University of Pittsburgh, 1973), 84–103; Jebb, "The Classical Renaissance," 554–55.

15. Roberto Weiss, "Learning and Education in Western Europe from 1470 to 1520," *New Cambridge Modern History* (Cambridge: Cambridge University Press, 1957), 1:95–96.

16. Arnaldo della Torre, *Storia dell'Accademia Platonica di Firenze* (Florence: Tipi G. Carmesecchi e figli, 1902), 176–203; Albert Castelnau, *Les Medicis*, (Paris, 1879) 1:148–65.

17. Arthur Tilley, *Studies in the French Renaissance* (Cambridge: Cambridge University Press, 1922), 188–254.

18. As quoted in Preserved Smith, *Erasmus* (New York: Harper and Bros., 1923), 29.

19. Paul Delannoy, *L'Université de Louvain, Conferences donnés au College de France en février, 1915* (Paris: Auguste Picard, 1915); Felix Neve, *La Renaissance des lettres et l'essor de l'erudition ancienne en Belgique,* (Louvain, 1890); Preserved Smith, *The Age of the Reformation* (New York: Henry Holt & Co., 1920), 663–73.

20. Ulrich von Hutten et al., *Epistolae obscurorum virorum,* Latin text with an English rendering, notes, and a historical introduction by Francis Griffin Stokes (New Haven, Conn.: Yale University Press, 1925); H. Ott and J. M. Fletcher, *The Medieval Statutes of the Faculty of Arts of the University of Freiburg-im-Breisgau* (Notre Dame, Ind.: University of Notre Dame, 1964), 11–125; George Kaufmann, *Die Geschichte der deutschen universitaten* (Stuttgart: I. G. Cotta'sche Buchhandlung, 1888), 2:486–550.

21. *Dictionary of National Biography,* eds. Sir Leslie Stephen and Sir Sidney Lee (London: Oxford University Press, 1922), 7: 58–59; 8:709–11; Roberto Weiss, *Humanism in England During the Fifteenth Century* (Oxford: Blackwell, 1967), 160–79.

22. Douglas Bush, *The Renaissance and English Humanism* (Toronto: University of Toronto Press, 1939), 79; on this point also see B. Groethuysen, "Renaissance," *Encyclopedia of the Social Sciences* 13 (1937), 281–82.

23. Charles Henry Cooper, *Annals of Cambridge* (Cambridge: Warwick and Co., 1845), 2:ͻ6; Thomas Nashe, *Pierce Penilesse, His Supplication to the Devil* (1592), ed. G. B. Harrison (New York: Barnes & Noble, 1966), 24–25; Foster Watson, *The Old Grammar Schools* (Cambridge: Cambridge University Press, 1916), 117–18.

24. John Steegman, *Cambridge* (London: B. T. Batsford, 1940), 14; Samuel Eliot Morison, *The Founding of Harvard College* (Cambridge, Mass.: Harvard University Press, 1935).

25. Stanley Lawrence Greenslade, ed. *The Work of William Tindale* (London: Blackie and Son, 1938), 93.

26. Joan Simon, *Education and Society in Tudor England* (Cambridge: Cambridge, University Press, 1967), 88; Margaret Mann Phillips, *Erasmus and the Northern Renaissance* (London: English Universities Press, 1959), 76–79.

27. As quoted in Jebb, "The Classical Renaissance," *Cambridge Modern History* 1 (1902):580–81.

28. Arnold J. Toynbee, *A Study of History,* vol. 12, *Reconsiderations (New York:* Oxford University Press, 1961), 530.

29. Lynn Thorndike, *A Short History of Civilization* (New York: Appleton-Century-Crofts, 1948), 352–54, 472; A. C. Crombie, *Augustine to Galileo* (London: William Heinemann, 1952), p. 373; George Sarton, *The Appreciation of Ancient and Medieval Science During the Renaissance* (Philadelphia: University of Pennsylvania Press, 1955), 170–71.

30. Wilhelm Windelband, *A History of Philosophy* (New York: Macmillan, 1893), p. 366.

31. Francis Bacon, *The Advancement of Learning* (New York: Willey Book Co., 1944), 2:59.

Chapter 3

1. John M. Todd *Martin Luther*, (Westminster, Md.: New Press, 1965), 120–22.
2. Roland Bainton, *Here I Stand A Life of Martin Luther*, (New York: Abingdon Press, 1970), 82–87; Heinrich Boehmer, *Road to Reformation: Martin Luther to the Year 1521*, (Philadelphia: Muhlenberg Press, 1946), 190–91; Edith Simon, *Luther Alive*, (Garden City, N.Y.: Doubleday & Co., 1968), 134–37.
3. Bainton, *Here I Stand*, 106; J. Verres, *Luther, An Historical Portrait*, (London: Burns and Oates, 1884), 62–63.
4. Bainton, *Here I Stand*, 107–8; Leopold von Ranke, *History of the Reformation in Germany*, (New York: Frederick Ungar, 1966), 1:199–200.
5. von Ranke, *History of the Reformation* 1:201–12.
6. Howard Kaminsky, "The University of Prague in the Hussite Revolution," in *Universities in Politics*, eds. John W. Baldwin and Richard A. Goldthwaite (Baltimore, Md.: Johns Hopkins Press, 1972), 79–106.
7. Preserved Smith, *The Age of the Reformation*, (New York: Henry Holt and Co., 1920), 149–57.
8. Smith, *Age of the Reformation*, 160–63.
9. John Steegman, *Cambridge*, (London: B. T. Batsford, 1940), 16–17; G. R. Elton, *Reform and Reformation*, (Cambridge, Mass.: Harvard University Press, 1977), 74–75.
10. von Ranke, *History of the Reformation* 1:288–91; Stephen d'Irsay, *Histoire des universitès francaises et étrangéres*, (Paris: Auguste Picard, 1935), 1:352–58; Denys Hay, "Schools and Universities," *New Cambridge Modern History* (Cambridge: Cambridge University Press, 1957), 2:431–37.
11. Lawrence Stone, ed., *The University in Society* (Princeton, N.J.: Princeton University Press, 1974), 1:16–23, 148–49, 202–19; John A. Venn, *Early Collegiate Life*, (Cambridge, England: W. Heffer & Sons, 1913); Lawrence P. Buck and Jonathan W. Zophy, eds., *The Social History of the Reformation*, (Columbus: Ohio State University Press, 1972), 249–65; Theodore G. Tappert, ed., *Luther: Letters of Spiritual Counsel* (Philadelphia: Westminster Press, 1955), 18:80–108.
12. Preserved Smith, *A History of Modern Culture* (Gloucester, Mass: Peter Smith, 1957), 1:329–37.
13. Steegman, *Cambridge*, 24–25.
14. Arnold J. Toynbee, *A Study of History*, vol. 12, *Reconsiderations* (New York: Oxford University Press, 1961), p. 530.
15. J. H. Elliott, *Europe Divided, 1559–1598*, (New York: Harper & Row, 1968), 40–41.
16. J. Simon, *Education and Society in Tudor England*, (Cambridge: Cambridge University Press, 1967), 197.
17. James B. Mullinger, *The University of Cambridge* (Cambridge: Cambridge University Press, 1884), 2:10–18, 24–197, 251–368; J. Simon, *Education and Society in Tudor England*, 199–215, 356–60.
18. *Statutes of the University of Cambridge*, (Cambridge: Cambridge University Press, 1914).

19. James Spedding, ed., *Francis Bacon's Works* (Boston: Houghton, Mifflin & Co., 1906), 8:82.

20. John Bruce and Thomas T. Perowne, eds., *The Correspondence of Matthew Parker*, (Cambridge: Cambridge University Press, 1843), 249.

21. William Harrison, *Elizabethan England*, Lathrop Withington, ed., introduction by F. J. Furnivall, (London: W. Scott Publishing Co., 1903), 261–62.

22. Mullinger, *University of Cambridge*, 2:79.

23. Ibid.

24. Johann C. A. Grohmann, *Annalen der Universität zu Wittenberg* (Meissen: 1801–1802), 1:152–56, as quoted in Mullinger, *University of Cambridge*, 105–6.

25. Hay, "Schools and Universities," 431–34.

26. Hay, "Schools and Universities," 427–29.

27. Wallace Notestein, *The English People on the Eve of Colonization, 1603–1630* (New York: Harper & Row, 1954), 140–42.

28. Simon, *Education in Tudor England*, 357–60.

29. Smith, *History of Modern Culture* 1:326–29.

30. Cecil J. Schneer, *The Search for Order*, (New York: Harper and Bros., 1960), 250–52.

31. P. Smith, *History of Modern Culture* 1:330.

32. P. Smith, *History of Modern Culture* 1:335.

33. P. Delaunay, "Intellectual Developments and the Reformation," in *The Beginnings of Modern Science*, ed. René Taton (New York: Basic Books, 1964), 167–71.

34. d'Irsay, *Histoire des universités* 1:311–38.

35. Mark H. Curtis, *Oxford and Cambridge in Transition*, (Oxford: Clarendon Press, 1959), 167–69.

36. A. L. Rowse, *The England of Elizabeth*, (New York: Macmillan Co., 1961), 518–23; Curtis, *Oxford and Cambridge in Transition*, 234–45.

37. Stephen F. Mason, *A History of the Sciences*, (New York: Collier Books, 1962), 176–77; Harold J. Grimm, *The Reformation Era, 1500–1650*, (New York: Macmillan Co., 1965), 594–95.

38. Curtis, *Oxford and Cambridge in Transition*, 234–45.

39. Grimm, *The Reformation Era*; Karl Holl, *The Cultural Significance of the Reformation*, (New York: Meridian Books, 1959); P. Smith, *Age of the Reformation*; Elliott, *Europe Divided*.

40. Delaunay, "Intellectual Developments and the Reformation," 167–68.

41. Wilhelm Windelband, *History of Philosophy*, (New York: Macmillan Co., 1893), 364–65; Alfred Weber and Ralph B. Perry, *History of Philosophy* (New York: Charles Scribner's Sons, 1896), 221–22; William H. Woodward, *Studies in Education During the Age of the Renaissance*, (New York: Russell and Russell, 1965), 214–33.

42. H. Richard Niebuhr, "The Reformation," *Encyclopaedia of the Social Sciences* 15:193.

Chapter 4

1. M. S. Anderson, *Europe in the Eighteenth Century, 1713–1783*, (New York: Holt, Rinehart and Winston, 1961), 288.

2. *The Ballad of Gresham College*, as quoted in A. R. Hall, *The Scientific Revolution, 1500–1800*, (London: Longmans, Green and Co., 1954), 187.

3. See *New Cambridge Modern History*, vol. 4, 1609–1659 (Cambridge: Cambridge University Press, 1970), 151–52.

4. David Ogg, *Europe of the Ancien Regime* (New York: Harper and Row, 1965), 313.

5. Leo Gershoy, *From Despotism to Revolution, 1765–1789* (New York: Harper and Bros., 1944), 284.

6. For the development of Oxford and Cambridge in the seventeenth and eighteenth centuries see Sir Charles E. Mallet, *A History of the University of Oxford*, vol. 3 (London: Methuen and Co., 1968) and James B. Mullinger, *The University of Cambridge*, vol. 2 (Cambridge: Cambridge University Press, 1884).

7. Maurice Ashley, *Great Britain to 1688* (Ann Arbor: University of Michigan Press, 1961), 390.

8. Herbert MacLachlan, *English Education Under the Test Acts* (Manchester, England: Manchester University Press, 1931).

9. Robert K. Merton, "Science, Technology, and Society in Seventeenth-Century England," *Osiris*, 4 (1938), 476–78.

10. George Rudé, *Europe in the Eighteenth Century* (New York: Praeger Publishers, 1972), 168; Vivian H. H. Green, *The Universities*. (Hammondsworth, England: Penguin Books, 1969), 99.

11. Stephen F. Mason, *A History of the Sciences* (New York: Collier Books, 1962), 284–85.

12. Gershoy, *From Despotism to Revolution*, 275.

13. Stephen d'Irsay, "Universities and Colleges," *Encyclopedia of the Social Sciences* 15:183; Theodore Zeldin, *France, 1848–1945*, 2, (Oxford: Clarendon Press, 1977), p.316.

14. Augustin Sicard, *Les études classiques avant la Revolution* (Paris: Perrin et cie, 1887).

15. René Taton, "The Rise of Analysis," in *The Beginnings of Modern Science* (New York: Basic Books, 1963), 397–98.

16. A. C. Crombie and Michael Hoskin, "The Scientific Movement and Its Influence, 1610–1650," *New Cambridge Modern History*, 4:43–44.

17. For more on this see J. L. Price, *Culture and Society in the Dutch Republic During the 17th Century* (London: B. T. Batsford, 1974), 203–8; also Peter Geyl, *The Netherlands in the Seventeenth Century: Part 2, 1648–1715* (New York: Barnes & Noble, 1964), 227–28.

18. J. D. Bernal, ed., *Science in History* (Cambridge, Mass.: M.I.T. Press, 1965), 2:512.

19. John T. Merz, *A History of European Scientific Thought in the Nineteenth Century* (New York: Dover Publications, 1965), 1:272.

20. David B. Horn, *A Short History of the University of Edinburgh*. (Edinburgh: Edinburgh University Press, 1967), 40–56.

21. Rosalind Mitchison, *A History of Scotland* (London: Methuen & Co., 1970), 332.

22. Horn, *Short History of the University of Edinburgh*, 41–42.

23. Merz, *History of European Scientific Thought* 1:269–73.

24. Nicholas Phillipson, "Culture and Society in the 18th-Century Province: The Case of Edinburgh and the Scottish Enlightenment," in *The University in Society*, ed. Lawrence Stone, (Princeton, N.J.: Princeton University Press, 1974), 2:410–11; 448.

25. Horn, *Short History of the University of Edinburgh*, 65.

26. A. R. Riggs, "The Colonial American Student at Edinburgh," *University of Edinburgh Journal* 20 (1961), 142–44; Whitney J. Bell, "Some American Students of . . . Dr. William Cullen of Edinburgh, 1755–1766," *Proceedings of the American Philosophical Society* 94:274–80.

27. J. H. Elliott, *Europe Divided, 1559–1598* (New York: Harper & Row, 1968), 77.

28. Marc Raeff, "The Well-Ordered Police State and the Development of Modernity in Seventeenth and Eighteenth Century Europe," *American Historical Review* 80 (December 1975), 1232.

29. Sir Adolphus Ward, "German Universities During and After the Thirty Years' War," in *Collected Papers* (Cambridge: Cambridge University Press, 1921), 1:195–202.

30. Carl Hinrichs, *Friedrich Wilhelm I* (Hamburg: Hanseatische Verlagsanstalt, 1941), 533–60.

31. Merton, "Science, Technology, and Society," 483–84.

32. W. H. Bruford, *Germany in the Eighteenth Century* (Cambridge, England: University Press, 1965), 242–43; M. Ornstein, *The Role of Scientific Societies in the Seventeenth Century* (Hamden, Conn.: Archon Books, 1963), 232–34; William Schrader, *Geschichte der Friedrichs-Universitat zu Halle*, (Berlin: F. Dümmler, 1894), 2:350–67.

33. Friedrich Paulsen, *German Education, Past and Present* (London: T. F. Unwin, 1908), 104–10, 122–23.

34. Charles E. McClelland, *State, Society, and University in Germany, 1700–1914* (Cambridge: Cambridge University Press, 1980), 34–35.

35. Paulsen, *German Education*, 120–33.

36. Francis L. Carsten, *The Origins of Prussia* (Oxford: Clarendon Press, 1954), 175–83; 255–60; Hans Rosenberg, *Bureaucracy, Aristocracy, and Autocracy: The Prussian Experience* (Cambridge, Mass.: Harvard University Press, 1966).

37. Gershoy, *From Despotism to Revolution*, 283.

38. Ogg, *Europe of the Ancien Regime*, 313.

39. Saul Padover, *The Revolutionary Emperor: Joseph II Of Austria* (Hamden, Conn.: Archon Books, 1967), 188–89.

40. Frederick Hertz, *The Development of the German Public Mind*, vol. 2 (London: Allen & Unwin, 1962).

41. McClelland, *State, Society, and University in Germany*, 47–49.

42. A. C. Crombie and Michael Hoskin, "The Scientific Movement, 1688–1751," *New Cambridge Modern History* 6:142–44.

43. Bruford, *Germany in the Eighteenth Century*, 243–46; R. Steven Turner, "University Reforms and Professional Scholarship in Germany, 1760–1806," in *The University in Society*, ed. Lawrence Stone 1:520; McClelland, *State, Society, and University*, 42–45.

44. See McClelland, *State, Society, and University*, 56–57.

45. Rosenberg, *Bureaucracy, Aristocracy, and Autocracy*, 180.

46. Helen P. Liebel, "Enlightened Bureaucracy *versus* Enlightened Despotism in Baden, 1750–1792," *Transactions of the American Philosophical Society*, N.S. 55 (1965), 21–22.

47. Gershoy, *From Despotism to Revolution*, 282.

Chapter 5

1. M. S. Anderson, *The Ascendancy of Europe* (Totowa, N.J.: Rowan & Littlefield, 1972), 136.

2. Leo Gershoy, *The French Revolution and Napoleon* (New York: F. S. Crofts & Co., 1947), 313–15; *New Cambridge Modern History* (Cambridge: Cambridge University Press, 1965), 8:169–73.

3. Terry Nicholas Clark, *The French University and the Emergence of the Social Sciences* (Cambridge, Mass.: Harvard University Press, 1973), 18.

4. Gershoy, *French Revolution and Napoleon*, 464–65.

5. Clark, *The French University*, 20.

6. Paul A. Gagnon, *France Since 1789* (New York: Harper & Row, 1964), 62–63; John Roach, "Education and the Press" in *New Cambridge Modern History* (Cambridge: Cambridge University Press, 1960), 10:115–16.

7. Stephen d'Irsay, "Universities and Colleges," *Encyclopedia of the Social Sciences* 15 (1934), 183.

8. Charles E. McClelland, *State, Society, and University in Germany, 1700–1914* (Cambridge: Cambridge University Press, 1980), 122–28, 142–43; John Roach, "Education and Public Opinion," in *New Cambridge Modern History* (Cambridge: Cambridge University Press, 1965), 9:195–96; Hajo Holborn, *A History of Modern Germany, 1648–1840* (New York: Alfred A. Knopf, 1964), 482–83.

9. Erich J. C. Hahn, "The Junior Faculty in 'Revolt,'" *American Historical Review* 82 (October 1977), 876–77.

10. McClelland, *State, Society, and University in Germany*, 146–47; Hahn, "The Junior Faculty in 'Revolt,'" 877.

11. William M. Johnston, *The Austrian Mind* (Berkeley: University of California Press, 1972), 69.

12. As quoted in C. A. Macartney, *The Hapsburg Empire, 1790–1918* (New York: Macmillan, 1969), 212.

13. Macartney, *The Hapsburg Empire,* 212–14.

14. Frederick B. Artz, *Reaction and Revolution, 1814–1832* (New York: Harper & Bros., 1934), 103.

15. K. H. Jarausch, "The Sources of German Student Unrest, 1815–1848," in *The University in Society,* ed. Lawrence Stone, (Princeton, N.J.: Princeton University Press, 1974), 2:537–38.

16. Koppel S. Pinson, *Modern Germany* (New York: Macmillan, 1966), 63–65.

17. Holborn, *History of Modern Germany,* 465–66.

18. Lenore O'Boyle, "The Problem of an Excess of Educated Men in Western Europe, 1800–1850," *Journal of Modern History* (December 1970), 42:475–78.

19. Stephen d'Irsay, *Histoire des universités francaises et étrangères,* (Paris: Auguste Picard, 1935), 2:257–58; Theodore Zeldin, *France, 1848–1945* (Oxford: Clarendon Press, 1977), 2:340.

20. Jarausch, "Sources of German Student Unrest," 541–50.

21. Arthur J. May, *Age of Metternich,* (New York: Holt, Rinehart, & Winston, 1963), 73.

22. Jarausch, "Sources of German Student Unrest," 449–50; John R. Gillis, *The Prussian Bureaucracy in Crisis, 1840–1860* (Stanford, Calif.: Stanford University Press, 1971), 12–55.

23. Priscilla Robertson, *Revolutions of 1848* (New York: Harper & Row, 1952), 180–82; 201–26; Hahn, "The Junior Faculty in 'Revolt,'" 880–94.

24. Gordon A. Craig, *Germany, 1866–1945* (New York: Oxford University Press, 1978), 200–210; McClelland, *State, Society, and University in Germany,* pp. 220–25.

25. Hugh Seton-Watson, *The Decline of Imperial Russia, 1855–1914* (New York: Praeger, 1956), 18–22; J. L. H. Keep, "Russia," in *New Cambridge Modern History* (Cambridge: Cambridge University Press, 1965), 9:358–59.

26. Seton-Watson, *Decline of Imperial Russia,* 21.

27. Nicholas Hans, *History of Russian Educational Policy, 1701–1917* (New York: Russell & Russell, 1964), 146–47.

28. Nicholas Hans, *The Russian Tradition in Education* (London: Routledge & Kegan Paul, 1963), 59–60; Seton-Watson, *Decline of Imperial Russia,* 56–57, 134–35; Hans, *Russian Educational Policy,* 142–45.

29. Sir Bernard Pares, "The Reform Movement in Russia," in *New Cambridge Modern History* (Cambridge: Cambridge University Press, 1934), 12:356–59; Hans, *Russian Educational Policy,* 172–204.

30. Artz, *Reaction and Revolution, 1814–1832,* 228–29; Guy Chapman, *The Third Republic of France* (New York: St. Martin's Press, 1962), 150–52; Gagnon, *France Since 1789,* 161.

31. Zeldin, *France* 2:320–21; Chapman, *Third Republic,* 166–168.

32. Elie Halevy, *The Triumph of Reform* (New York: Barnes & Noble, 1961), 197–202; E. L. Woodward, *The Age of Reform, 1815–1870* (Oxford: Oxford University Press, 1938), 470–71.

33. Vivian H. H. Green, *The Universities* (Hammondsworth, England: Penguin Books, 1969), 103–6; Artz, *Reaction and Revolution,* 101–2.

34. George M. Trevelyan, *British History in the Nineteenth Century, 1782–1901* (New York: Longmans, Green, and Co., 1922) 354–56; Robert C. K. Ensor, *England, 1870–1914* (Oxford: Clarendon Press, 1936), 147–48; Woodward, *The Age of Reform*, 472–73.

35. A. Victor Murray, "Education," *New Cambridge Modern History*, Vol. 11, (Cambridge, England: University Press, 1962) 183–84; John B. Mullinger, "Universities," *Encyclopedia Britttanica* (eleventh ed.) 7:767.

36. B. H. M. Vlekke, "Education," B. Landheer, ed. *The Netherlands* (Berkeley: University of California Press, 1946), 234.

37. Murray, "Education," 182.

38. Paul L. Robertson, "The Finances of the University of Glasgow Before 1914," *History of Education Quarterly* 16 (Winter 1976):474–75.

39. Gillis, *Prussian Bureaucracy*, 200–201.

40. Fritz Ringer, *The Decline of the German Mandarins* (Cambridge, Mass.: Harvard University Press, 1969), 26.

41. As quoted in Ringer, *Decline of the German Mandarins*, 34–35.

42. Ensor, *England, 1870–1914*, 22–23; 148–50; 321–23; 537–38.

43. Green, *The Universities*, 97–98; 117.

44. Murray G. Ross, *The University: The Anatomy of Academe* (New York: McGraw-Hill, 1976), 37.

45. Trevelyan, *British History*, 355.

46. Memorandum of the Oxford University Extension Delegacy, Vol. 5 (1894), pp. 289–95 as quoted in Elie Halevy, *Imperialism and the Rise of Labor* (New York: Barnes & Noble, 1961), 191.

47. Anderson, *Ascendancy of Europe*, 136.

48. Mullinger, "Universities," 769.

49. Jean C. Bracq, *France Under the Republic* (London: T. Werner Laurie, 1910), 80.

50. Sidney Webb, "Social Movements," in *Cambridge Modern History*, Vol. 12 (Cambridge: Cambridge University Press, 1934), 762

51. Hans, *Russian Educational Policy*, 109-10; Roach, "Education and the Press," 119.

52. Seton-Watson, *Decline of Imperial Russia*, 57–58; Hans, *Russian Educational Policy*, 147–48; 175; 200–205.

53. Craig. *Germany*, 418–19; McClelland, *State, Society, and University in Germany*, 250.

54. Johnston, *The Austrian Mind*, 71.

55. Roach, "Education and the Press," 119–120; Elie Halevy, *The Rule of Democracy* (London: Ernest Benn, 1952), 502.

56. Ensor, *England, 1870–1914*, 149–50.

57. Murray, "Education," 197–99.

58. C. C. Gillispie, "Science and Technology," in *New Cambridge Modern History* (Cambridge: Cambridge University Press, 1965), 9:123.

59. Gillispie, "Science and Technology," 122; Gagnon, *France Since 1789*, 62.

60. Zeldin, *France* 2:339–41.

61. Bracq, *France Under the Republic*, 81–82; L. Pearce Williams, "Science, Educa-

tion, and Napoleon," *Isis* 47 (December 1956), 375–81.

62. Roach, "Education and the Press," 115–16.

63. Zeldin, *France* 2:323–42.

64. For a discussion of the Technische Hochschulen, see Eric Ashby, *Technology and the Academies* (London: Macmillan, 1959), 59–61; Ringer, *Decline of the German Mandarins*, 28, 39, 51–58; McClelland, *State, Society, and University in Germany*, 236–37, 284–87, 300–302, has material on the research institutes.

65. John Theodore Merz, *A History of European Scientific Thought in the Nineteenth Century* (New York: Dover Publications, 1965), 1:167.

66. Holborn, *History of Modern Germany*, 479.

67. Friedrich Paulsen, *The German Universities and University Study* (New York: Charles Scribner's Sons, 1906), 40–43.

68. McClelland, *State, Society, and University in Germany*, 172–73.

69. Merz, *Scientific Thought* 1:188.

70. Reginald H. Phelps, "The Idea of the Modern University: Göttingen and America," *Germanic Review* 29 (October 1954), 184–86; McClelland, *State, Society, and University in Germany*, 20, 174–75.

71. Gillispie, "Science and Technology," 129.

72. Ashby, *Technology and the Academies*, 28–31.

73. J. D. Bernal, ed., *Science in History* (Cambridge, Mass.: M.I.T. Press, 1965), 2:552–53.

74. Green, *The Universities*, 100.

75. A. H. Halsey and M. A. Trow, *The British Academics* (London: Faber and Faber, 1971), 54.

76. Green, *The Universities*, 112–20.

77. Murray, "Education," 196.

78. Ensor, *England, 1870–1914*, 538.

79. Halevy, *Imperialism and the Rise of Labor*, 146.

80. Murray, "Education," 182; Green, *The Universities*, 117–19.

81. Robert G. McPherson, *Theory of Higher Education in Nineteenth-Century England* (Athens: University of Georgia Press, 1959), 103–14; Ashby, *Technology and the Academies*, 32–39; Woodward, *Age of Reform*, 472–73.

Chapter 6

1. Stephen D'Irsay, "Universities and Colleges," *Encyclopedia of the Social Sciences* 8 (1934), 184.

2. Mario Gongora, *Studies in the Colonial History of Spanish America* (Cambridge: Cambridge University Press, 1975), 187–90.

3. Murray G. Ross, *The University: The Anatomy of Academe* (New York: McGraw-Hill, 1976), 20–43.

4. John S. Brubacher and Willis Rudy, *Higher Education in Transition* (New York: Harper & Row, 1976), 3–23.

5. Eric Ashby, *Universities: British, Indian, African* (Cambridge, Mass.: Harvard

University Press, 1966); T. H. Silcock, *The South-east Asian University* (Durham, N.C.: Duke University Press, 1964), 3–67; Z. K. Matthews, *African Awakening and the Universities* (Capetown, S.A.: University of Capetown, 1961), 3–17.

6. Philip G. Altbach, ed., *University Reform* (Cambridge: Mass.: Schenkman Publishing Co., 1974), 65–66.

7. *New York Times*, 30 November 1976, 16.

8. Damodar P. Singhal, *India and World Civilization* (East Lansing: Michigan State University Press, 1969), 299.

9. Eric Ashby, *African Universities and Western Tradition* (Cambridge, Mass.: Harvard University Press, 1964), 94–96.

10. Ashby, *African Universities*, 94–96.

11. Latourette, *The Development of China*, (Boston: Houghton Mifflin, 1946), 275; Rhoads Murphey, *The Outsiders* (Ann Arbor: University of Michigan Press, 1977), 228–29.

12. José Ortega y Gasset, *Mission of the University* (New York: W. W. Norton & Co., 1944), 40.

Bibliography

Books

Adams, Marion, ed. *The German Tradition: Aspects of Art and Thought in the German-Speaking Countries.* Sydney, Australia: John Wiley and Sons, 1971.

Addy, George M. *The Enlightenment in the University of Salamanca.* Durham, N.C.: Duke University Press, 1966.

Allen, P. S. *The Age of Erasmus.* Oxford: Clarendon Press, 1914.

Altbach, Philip G., ed. *University Reform.* Cambridge, Mass.: Schenkman Publishing Co., 1974.

Anderson, M. S. *The Ascendancy of Europe.* Totowa, N.J.: Rowman and Littlefield, 1972.

Anderson, M. S. *Europe in the Eighteenth Century, 1713–1783.* New York: Holt, Rinehart and Winston, 1961.

Artz, Frederick B. *Reaction and Revolution, 1814–1832.* New York: Harper & Bros., 1934.

Ashby, Eric. *African Universities and Western Tradition.* Cambridge, Mass.: Harvard University Press, 1964.

Ashby, Eric. *Technology and the Academies.* London: Macmillan & Co., 1959.

Ashley, Maurice. *Great Britain to 1688.* Ann Arbor: University of Michigan Press, 1961.

Bainton, Roland. *Here I Stand: A Life of Martin Luther.* New York: Abingdon Press, 1970.

Baldwin, James W., and Goldthwaite, Richard A., eds. *Universities in Politics*. Baltimore, Md.: Johns Hopkins Press, 1972.

Barnard, H. C. *A History of English Education from 1760*. London: University of London Press, 1964.

Barnes, Harry Elmer. *An Intellectual and Cultural History of the Western World*. Vol. 1. New York: Dover Publications, 1963.

Ben-David, Joseph. *Centers of Learning*. New York: McGraw-Hill Book Co., 1977.

Bernal, J. D., ed. *Science in History*. Vol. 2. Cambridge, Mass.: M.I.T. Press, 1965.

Bockstael, Eric, and Feinstein, Otto. *Higher Education in the European Community*. Lexington, Mass.: D.C. Heath and Co., 1970.

Boehmer, Heinrich. *Road to Reformation: Martin Luther to the Year 1521*. Philadelphia: Muhlenberg Press, 1946.

Bowen, James. *A History of Western Education*. Vols. 1 and 2. New York: St. Martin's Press, 1972, 1975.

Brucker, Gene. *Renaissance Florence*. New York: John Wiley & Sons, 1969.

Bruford, W. H. *Germany in the Eighteenth Century*. Cambridge, England: The University Press, 1965.

————. *Culture and Society in Classical Weimar, 1775–1806*. Cambridge, Mass.: The University Press, 1962.

Buck, Lawrence P., and Zophy, Jonathan W., eds.: *The Social History of the Reformation*. Columbus: Ohio State University Press, 1972.

Buckland, Georgina. "Byzantine Education." In *Byzantium*, ed. Norman H. Baynes and H. St. L. B. Moss. London: Oxford University Press, 1948.

Burn, Barbara B., et. al. *Higher Education in Nine Countries*. New York: McGraw-Hill Book Co., 1971.

Bush, Douglas. *The Renaissance and English Humanism*. Toronto: University of Toronto Press, 1939.

Cambridge Modern History. Vol. 5. New York: Macmillan Co., 1934.

Carr, Raymond. *Spain, 1808–1939*. Oxford: Clarendon Press, 1966.

Chapman, Guy. *The Third Republic of France*. New York: St. Martin's Press, 1962.

Cheyney, Edward P. *The Dawn of a New Era, 1250–1453*. New York: Harper & Row, 1936.

Clark, Donald L. *Rhetoric in Greco-Roman Education*. New York: Columbia University Press, 1957.

Clark, George. *The Seventeenth Century*. Oxford: Clarendon Press, 1929.

Clark, Terry N. *The French University and the Emergence of the Social Sciences*. Cambridge, Mass.: Harvard University Press, 1973.

Compayre, Gabriel. *Abelard and the Origin and Early History of Universities*. New York: Charles Scribner's Sons, 1893.

Cragg, Gerald R. *The Church and the Age of Reason, 1648–1789*. New York: Atheneum, 1961.

Craig, Gordon A. *Germany, 1866–1945*. New York: Oxford University Press, 1978.

Crombie, A. C. *Augustine to Galileo*. London: William Heinemann, 1952.

Curtis, Mark H. *Oxford and Cambridge in Transition, 1558–1642*. Oxford: Clarendon Press, 1959.

Daly, Lowrie J. *The Medieval University, 1200–1400*. New York: Sheed and Ward, 1961.

Davie, George E. *The Democratic Intellect*. Edinburgh: University of Edinburgh Press, 1962.

Dickens, A. G. *The Counter Reformation*. New York: Harcourt, Brace & World, 1969.

Dorwart, Reinhold A. *The Administrative Reforms of Frederick William I of Prussia*. Cambridge, Mass.: Harvard University Press, 1953.

———. *The Prussian Welfare State Before 1740*. Cambridge, Mass.: Harvard University Press, 1971.

Dresden, S. *Humanism in the Renaissance*. New York: McGraw-Hill Book Co., 1968.

Durant, Will. *The Renaissance*. New York: Simon and Schuster, 1953.

———. *The Reformation*. New York: Simon and Schuster, 1957.

Durant, Ariel and Will. *The Age of Voltaire*. New York: Simon and Schuster, 1965.

Elton, G. R. *Reform and Reformation, England: 1509–1558.* Cambridge, Mass.: Harvard University Press, 1977.

Ensor, Robert C. K. *England, 1870–1914.* Oxford: Clarendon Press, 1936.

Erasmus, Desiderius. *The Correspondence of Erasmus.* R. A. B. Mynors and D. F. S. Thomson, trans., Toronto. University of Toronto Press, 1974.

Fehl, Noah E. *The Idea of a University in East and West.* Hong Kong: Chung Chi College, 1962.

Gagliardo, John G. *Enlightened Despotism.* New York: Thomas Y. Crowell Co., 1967.

Gagnon, Paul A. *France Since 1789.* New York: Harper & Row, 1964.

Gershoy, Leo. *From Despotism to Revolution, 1765–1789,* New York: Harper & Bros., 1944.

———. *The French Revolution and Napoleon.* New York: F. S. Crofts & Co., 1947.

Geyl, Peter. *The Netherlands in the Seventeenth Century.* Part 2, *1648–1715.* New York: Barnes & Noble, 1964.

Gillis, John R. *The Prussian Bureaucracy in Crisis, 1840–1860.* Stanford, Calif.: Stanford University Press, 1971.

Gilmore, Myron P. *The World of Humanism, 1453–1517.* New York: Harper & Row, 1952.

Green, Vivian H. H. *The Universities.* Hammondsworth, England: Penguin Books, 1969.

Halevy, Elie. *Imperialism and the Rise of Labor.* New York: Barnes & Noble, 1961.

———. *The Rule of Democracy.* London: Ernest Benn, 1952.

———. *The Triumph of Reform.* New York: Barnes & Noble, 1961.

Hall, A. R. *The Scientific Revolution, 1500–1800.* London: Longmans, Green and Co., 1954.

Halsey, Albert H., and Trow, M. A. *The British Academics.* London: Faber and Faber, 1971.

Hans, Nicholas A. *Comparative Education.* London: Routledge & Kegan Paul, 1950.

———. *History of Russian Educational Policy, 1701–1917.* New York: Russell & Russell, 1964.

————. *The Russian Tradition in Education.* London: Routledge & Kegan Paul, 1963.

Harris, Ronald W. *Absolutism and Enlightenment, 1660–1789.* London: Blandford Press, 1967.

Haskins, Charles H. *The Rise of Universities.* Ithaca, N.Y.: Cornell University Press, 1957.

————. *Studies in Medieval Culture.* New York: Frederick Ungar Publishing Co., 1965.

Hayden, Howard. *Higher Education and Development in South-East Asia.* Paris: UNESCO, 1967.

Hearnshaw, F. J. C., ed. *Medieval Contributions to Modern Civilization.* London: George G. Harrap, 1921.

Hertz, Frederick. *The Development of the German Public Mind.* Vol. 2. London: Allen & Unwin, 1962.

Hess, Gerhard. *Universities in Germany, 1930–1970.* Bad Godesberg: Inter Nationes, 1968.

Hinrichs, Carl. *Friedrich Wilhelm I.* Hamburg: Hanseatische Verlagsanstalt, 1941.

Holborn, Hajo. *A History of Modern Germany, 1648–1840.* New York: Alfred A. Knopf, 1964.

Holl, Karl. *The Cultural Significance of the Reformation.* New York: Meridian Books, 1959.

Horn, David B. *A Short History of the University of Edinburgh.* Edinburgh: University of Edinburgh Press, 1967.

Houghton, Walter E. *The Victorian Frame of Mind, 1830–1870.* New Haven, Conn.: Yale University Press, 1957.

Hovde, B. J. *The Scandinavian Countries.* Vol. 2. Boston: Chapman & Grimes, 1943.

Huizinga, Johann. *Erasmus and the Age of the Reformation.* New York: Harper & Bros., 1957.

Hussey, J. M. *Church and Learning in the Byzantine Empire, 867–1185.* New York: Russell & Russell, 1963.

d'Irsay, Stephen. *Histoire des universités francaises et étrangères.* Vols. 1 and 2. Paris: Auguste Picard, 1935.

Jaeger, Werner. *Paideia: The Ideals of Greek Culture.* Vol. 1. New York: Oxford University Press, 1945.

Johnson, William H. E. *Russia's Educational Heritage*. Pittsburgh, Pa.: Carnegie Press, 1950.

Johnston, William M. *The Austrian Mind*. Berkeley: University of California Press, 1972.

Jones, Richard F. *Ancients and Moderns*. St. Louis, Mo.: Washington University Press, 1961.

Junge, Gerhard. *The Universities of Indonesia*. Bremen: Bremen Economic Research Society, 1973.

Kann, Robert A. *A Study in Austrian Intellectual History*. New York: Octagon Books, 1973.

Kibre, Pearl. *Scholarly Privileges in the Middle Ages*. Cambridge, Mass.: Medieval Academy of America, 1962.

King, Richard G. *The Provincial Universities of Mexico*. New York: Praeger Publishers, 1971.

Klette, Theodor. *Beiträge zur Geschichte und Literatur der Italienischen Gelehrteurenaissance*. Hildesheim: G. Olms, 1970.

Kohn, Hans. *The Twentieth Century: The Challenge to the West and Its Response*. New York: Macmillan Co., 1957.

Kossmann, E. H. *The Low Countries, 1780–1940*. Oxford: Clarendon Press, 1978.

Kotschnig, Walter M., ed. *The University in a Changing World*. London: Oxford University Press, 1932.

Kristeller, Paul Oskar. *Renaissance Thought*. New York: Harper & Row, 1961.

Lanning, John Tate. *The Eighteenth-Century Enlightenment in the University of San Carlos de Guatemala*. Ithaca, N.Y.: Cornell University Press, 1956.

Latourette, Kenneth S. *The Chinese: Their History and Culture*. New York: Macmillan Co., 1964.

———. *The Development of China*. Boston: Houghton Mifflin, 1946.

Laurie, S. S. *The Rise and Early Constitution of Universities*. New York: D. Appleton and Co., 1887.

Leff, Gordon. *Paris and Oxford Universities in the 13th and 14th Centuries*. New York: John Wiley & Sons, 1968.

Liard, Louis. *Universités et Facultes*. Paris: A. Colin et cie, 1890.

Lilge, Frederic. *The Abuse of Learning*. New York: Octagon Books, 1975.

Lopez, Robert S. *The Three Ages of the Italian Renaissance*. Charlottesville: University of Virginia Press, 1970.

Macartney, C. A. *The Hapsburg Empire, 1790–1918*. New York: Macmillan Co., 1969.

McClelland, Charles E. *State, Society, and University in Germany, 1700–1914*. Cambridge: Cambridge University Press, 1980.

McClelland, Charles E., and Scher, Steven P., eds. *Postwar German Culture*. New York: E. P. Dutton & Co., 1974.

McPherson, Robert G. *Theory of Higher Education in Nineteenth-Century England*. Athens: University of Georgia Press, 1959.

McRoberts, David, ed. *Essays on the Scottish Reformation*. Glasgow: Burns, 1962.

Majumbar, R. C., ed. *The Age of Imperial Unity*. Bombay: Bharatiya Vidya Bhavan, 1951.

Mallet, Charles E. *A History of the University of Oxford*. Vol. 3. London: Methuen and Co., 1968.

Mason, Stephen F. *A History of the Sciences*. New York: Collier Books, 1962.

Mathew, David. *The Social Structure in Caroline England*. Oxford: Clarendon Press, 1948.

Matthews, Z. K. *African Awakening and the Universities*. Cape Town, S.A.: University of Cape Town, 1961.

May, Arthur J. *The Hapsburg Monarchy, 1867–1914*. Cambridge, Mass.: Harvard University Press, 1965.

Merz, John T. *A History of European Scientific Thought in the Nineteenth Century*. Vol. 1. New York: Dover Publications, 1965.

Mitchison, Rosalind. *A History of Scotland*. London: Methuen & Co., 1970.

Morison, Samuel Eliot. *The Founding of Harvard College*. Cambridge, Mass.: Harvard University Press, 1935.

Mousnier, Roland. *Social Hierarchies*. New York: Schocken Books, 1973.

Mullinger, James B. *The University of Cambridge*. Vol. 2. Cambridge: Cambridge University Press, 1884.

Murphey, Rhoads. *The Outsiders*. Ann Arbor: University of Michigan Press, 1977.

Needham, Joseph. *Science and Civilization in China*. Vol. 1. Cambridge: Cambridge University Press, 1954.

————. *Science and Civilization in China*. Vol. 2. Cambridge: Cambridge University Press, 1969.

New Cambridge Modern History. 12 vols. Cambridge: Cambridge University Press. Vol. 1, *The Renaissance* (1957); vol. 2, *The Reformation* (1958); vol. 4, *1609–1659* (1970), vol. 6, *1688–1725* (1970); vol. 11, *1870–1898* (1962); vol. 12, *1898–1945* (1960).

New Cambridge Modern History. Vol. 1, *The Renaissance*. Cambridge: Cambridge University Press, 1957.

New Cambridge Modern History. Vol. 2, *The Reformation*. Cambridge: The University Press, 1958.

New Cambridge Modern History. Vol. 4, *1609–1659*. Cambridge: Cambridge University Press, 1970.

New Cambridge Modern History. Vol. 6, *1688–1725*. Cambridge: Cambridge University Press, 1970.

New Cambridge Modern History. Vol. 11, *1870–1898*. Cambridge: Cambridge University Press, 1962.

New Cambridge Modern History. Vol. 12, *1898–1945*. Cambridge: Cambridge University Press, 1960.

Newton, Gerald. *The Netherlands*. London: Ernest Benn, 1978.

Norton, Arthur O. *Readings in the History of Education: Medieval Universities*. Cambridge, Mass.: Harvard University Press, 1909.

Notestein, Wallace. *The English People on the Eve of Colonization, 1603–1630*. New York: Harper & Row, 1954.

Ogg, David. *Europe of the Ancien Régime, 1715–1783*. New York: Harper and Row, 1965.

Ortega y Gasset, José. *Mission of the University*. New York: W. W. Norton & Co., 1944.

Padover, Saul K. *The Revolutionary Emperor: Joseph II of Austria*. Hamden, Conn.: Archon Books, 1967.

Paetow, Louis John. *The Arts Course at Medieval Universities*. Urbana, Ill.: University of Illinois Press, 1910.

Parsons, Edward A. *The Alexandrian Library*. New York: American Elsevier Publishing Co., 1952.

Paulsen, Friedrich. *The German Universities and University Study.* New York: Charles Scribner's Sons, 1906.

Pinson, Koppel S. *Modern Germany.* New York: Macmillan, 1966.

Price, J. L. *Culture and Society in the Dutch Republic During the 17th Century.* London: B. T. Batsford, Ltd, 1974.

Prokofiev, M. A. *et al. Higher Education in the U.S.S.R.* Paris: Unesco, 1961.

Rabb, Theodore K., and Siegel, Jerrold E., eds. *Action and Conviction in Early Modern Europe.* Princeton N.J.: Princeton University Press, 1969.

Radcliffe-Umstead, Douglas, ed. *The University World: A Synoptic View of Higher Education.* Pittsburgh,: Pa. University of Pittsburgh, 1973.

Rait, Robert S. *Life in the Medieval University.* Cambridge: Cambridge University Press, 1912.

von Ranke, Leopold. *History of the Reformation in Germany.* New York: Frederick Ungar Publishing Co., 1966.

Rashdall, Hastings. *The Universities of Europe in the Middle Ages.* Vols. 2 and 3. Oxford: Clarendon Press, 1951.

Resposo, Epifania R. C. *The Role of Universities in the Developing Philippines.* New York: Asia Publishing House, 1971.

Ringer, Fritz K. *The Decline of the German Mandarins.* Cambridge, Mass.: Harvard University Press, 1969.

―――. *Education and Society in Modern Europe.* Bloomington: Indiana University Press, 1979.

Roberts, S. C. *British Universities.* London: Collins, 1947.

Robertson, Priscilla. *Revolutions of 1848.* New York: Harper & Row, 1952.

Rosenberg, Hans. *Bureaucracy, Aristocracy, and Autocracy: The Prussian Experience.* Cambridge, Mass.: Harvard University Press, 1966.

Ross, Murray G. *The University: The Anatomy of Academe.* New York: McGraw-Hill, 1976.

Rowse, A. L. *The England of Elizabeth.* New York: Macmillan Co., 1961.

Rudd, Ernest. *The Highest Education: A Study of Graduate Education in Britain.* London: Routledge & Kegan Paul, 1975.

Rudé, George. *Europe in the Eighteenth Century.* New York: Praeger Publishers, 1972.

Runciman, Steven. *The Last Byzantine Renaissance.* Cambridge: Cambridge University Press, 1970.

Sabbadini, Remigio. *Le Scoperte dei Codici Latini e Greci ne secoli XIV e XV.* Florence: G. C. Sansoni, 1967.

Sarton, George. *The Appreciation of Ancient and Medieval Science During the Renaissance.* Philadelphia: University of Pennsylvania Press, 1955.

Schachner, Nathan. *The Medieval Universities.* New York: A. S. Barnes & Co., 1962.

Schneer, Cecil J. *The Search for Order.* New York, Harper & Bros., 1960.

Scott, Franklin D. *Sweden: The Nation's History.* Minneapolis: University of Minnesota Press, 1977.

Seton-Watson, Hugh. *The Decline of Imperial Russia, 1855–1914.* New York: Praeger Publishers, 1956.

Seybolt, Robert F. *Manuale Scholarium.* Cambridge, Mass.: Harvard University, 1921.

Shaw, Stanford J., and Shaw, Ezel Kural. *History of the Ottoman Empire.* Vol. 2. Cambridge: Cambridge University Press, 1977.

Silcock, T. H. *The South-east Asian University.* Durham, N.C.: Duke University Press, 1964.

Simon, Edith. *Luther Alive.* Garden City, N.Y.: Doubleday & Co., 1968.

Simon, Joan. *Education and Society in Tudor England.* Cambridge: Cambridge University Press, 1967.

Simon, W. M. *Germany: A Brief History.* New York; Random House, 1966.

Smith, Preserved. *The Age of the Reformation.* New York: Henry Holt and Co., 1920.

———. *Erasmus.* New York: Harper & Bros., 1923.

———. *A History of Modern Culture,* Vol. 1. Gloucester, Mass.: Peter Smith, 1957.

Smith, William. *Ancient Education.* New York: Philosophical Library, 1955.

Smout, T. C. *A History of the Scottish People, 1560–1830*. New York: Charles Scribner's Sons, 1969.

Steegman, John. *Cambridge*. London: B. T. Batsford, 1940.

Stimie, C. M. *University Education in the Republic of South Africa*. Pretoria: South African Human Sciences Research Council, 1972.

Stobart, J. C. *The Grandeur That Was Rome*. London: Sidgwick and Jackson, 1961.

Stone, Lawrence, ed. *The University in Society*. Vols. 1 and 2. Princeton, N.J.: Princeton University Press, 1974.

Sumner, B. H. *A Short History of Russia*. New York: Harcourt, Brace and Company, 1949.

Thomas, John R., and Kruse-Vaucienne, Ursula, eds. *Soviet Science and Technology*. Washington, D.C.: George Washington University, 1977.

Thorndike, Lynn. *Science and Thought in the Fifteenth Century*. New York: Hafner Publishing Co., 1963.

Tilley, Arthur, ed. *Medieval France*. New York: Hafner Publishing Co., 1964.

Todd, John M. *Martin Luther*. Westminster, Md.: The Newman Press, 1965.

Toynbee, Arnold J. *A Study of History*. Vol. 12 *Reconsiderations*. New York: Oxford University Press, 1961.

Trevelyan, George M. *British History in the Nineteenth Century, 1782–1901*. New York: Longmans, Green and Co., 1922.

Verres, J. *Luther, An Historical Portrait*. London: Burns & Oates, 1884.

Walsh, James J. *The Thirteenth, Greatest of Centuries*. New York: AMS Press, 1970.

Weiss, Roberto. *Humanism in England During the Fifteenth Century*. Oxford, England: Blackwell, 1967.

Wolf, Abraham. *A History of Science, Technology, and Philosophy in the 16th and 17th Centuries*. London: Allen & Unwin, 1935.

———. *A History of Science, Technology, and Philosophy in the 18th Century*. London: Allen & Unwin, 1938.

Woodward, E. L. *The Age of Reform, 1815–1870*. Oxford, England: Oxford University Press, 1938.

Woodward, William H. *Studies in Education During the Age of the Renaissance*. New York: Russell & Russell, 1965.

Wright, Louis B. *Middle Class Culture in Elizabethan England*. Ithaca, N.Y.: Cornell University Press, 1958.

Zeldin, Theodore. France, 1848–1945. Vol. 2. Oxford: Clarendon Press, 1977.

Articles

Ashby, Eric. "Ivory Towers in Tomorrow's World." *Journal of Higher Education* 38 (November 1967:417–27.

Banker, James R. "The Ars Dictaminis and Rhetorical Textbooks at the Bolognese University in the Fourteenth Century." *Medievalia et Humanistica* n.s. 5 (1974):153–63.

Ben-David, Joseph. "Universities." *Encyclopedia of the Social Sciences* 16 (1968):191–98.

Destrez, J., and Chenu, M. D. "Exemplaria Universitaires des XIIIᵉ et XIVᵉ siecles." *Scriptorium* 7 1953:68–80.

Heath, Terrence. "Logical Grammar, Grammatical Logic, and Humanism in Three German Universities." *Studies in the Renaissance* 18 (1971):400–432.

d'Irsay, Stephen. "Universities and Colleges." *Encyclopedia of the Social Sciences* 15 (1934):181–85.

Liebel, Helen, P. "Enlightened Bureaucracy *versus* Enlightened Despotism in Baden, 1750–1792." *Transactions of the American Philosophical Society* n.s.55 (1965):20–22.

Marshall, Byron K. "The Tradition of Conflict in the Governance of Japan's Imperial Universities." *History of Education Quarterly* 17 (Winter 1977):385–403.

Merton, Robert K. "Science, Technology, and Society in Seventeenth-Century England." *Osiris* 4 (1938):465–90.

Mullinger, John B. "Universities." *Encyclopaedia Britannica* (11th edition), 17:750–69.

O'Boyle, Lenore. "The Problem of an Excess of Educated Men in Western Europe, 1800–1850." *Journal of Modern History* 42 (December 1970):475–94.

Ozment, Steven E. "The University and the Church, Patterns of Reform in Jean Gerson." *Medievalia et Humanistica* n.s.1 (1970):111–22.

Paul, Harry W. "Scholarship and Ideology: The Chair of the General History of Science at the College de France, 1892–1913." *Isis* 67 (September 1976):376–97.

Rashdall, Hastings. "The Medieval Universities." *The Cambridge Medieval History* 6 (1936):560–72.

Robertson, Paul L. "The Finances of the University of Glasgow Before 1914." *History of Education Quarterly* 16 (Winter 1976):470–81.

Thomas, Carla R. "Philosophical Anthropology and Educational Change: Wilhelm von Humboldt and the Prussian Reforms." *History of Education Quarterly* 13 (Fall 1973):219–29.

Index